YANKO TSVETKOV

Atlas²
OF PREJUDICE
VOLUME 2

The *Mapping Stereotypes* project developed from a satirical map of Europe made by Yanko Tsvetkov in 2009. After it became viral on the Internet, the author started expanding the initially spontaneous idea, focusing on national and historical prejudices, and stereotypes.

The project has been featured widely in the media all over the world: *BBC Radio*, *The Telegraph* and *The Guardian* newspapers in the UK; the *Rai Uno* TV, *Corriere della Sera* newspaper and *Focus* magazine in Italy; the *Izvestiya* newspaper in Russia; *The Times of India*; the *Süddeutsche Zeitung* in Germany; the *Aftenposten* newspaper in Norway; *Newsweek Polska* magazine in Poland; The *Daily Beast* and *Wired* in the USA; the regional editions of *GQ* magazine in Brazil and South Africa; the *Semana* magazine in Colombia; the *Sábado* magazine in Portugal; and many others.

The German *Stern* recognized it as "Satire of the Year" in its 2011 kaleidoscope edition.

After the publication of the German edition of the *Atlas of Prejudice* in February 2013, the newspaper *Die Zeit* described the project as "ironic and at the same time an effective contribution to cultural understanding." *Der Spiegel* magazine added, "Not since the creation of the Asterix comics have national prejudices entered our culture in such an entertaining way."

ATLAS OF PREJUDICE
VOLUME 2

First English edition: February 2014
Text, illustration, design, bells, and whistles by Yanko Tsvetkov
Typefaces: *Open Sans* by Steve Matteson, *PT Sans* and *PT Serif* by ParaType, *Roboto Slab* by Christian Robertson

Published by Alphadesigner in the United States of America
Copyright ©2014 Yanko Tsvetkov. All rights reserved
Printed by CreateSpace, an Amazon.com Company
Available from Amazon.com, CreateSpace.com, and other retail outlets

ISBN: 978-1495395871 (English paperback edition)

The book is also available in the following languages:

ISBN: 978-3868736922 (German hardcover edition, March 2014 by Knesebeck GmbH & Co. Verlag KG, Munich, Germany)

www.alphadesigner.com
www.atlasofprejudice.com
email: alphadesigner@gmail.com

CONTENT NETWORK

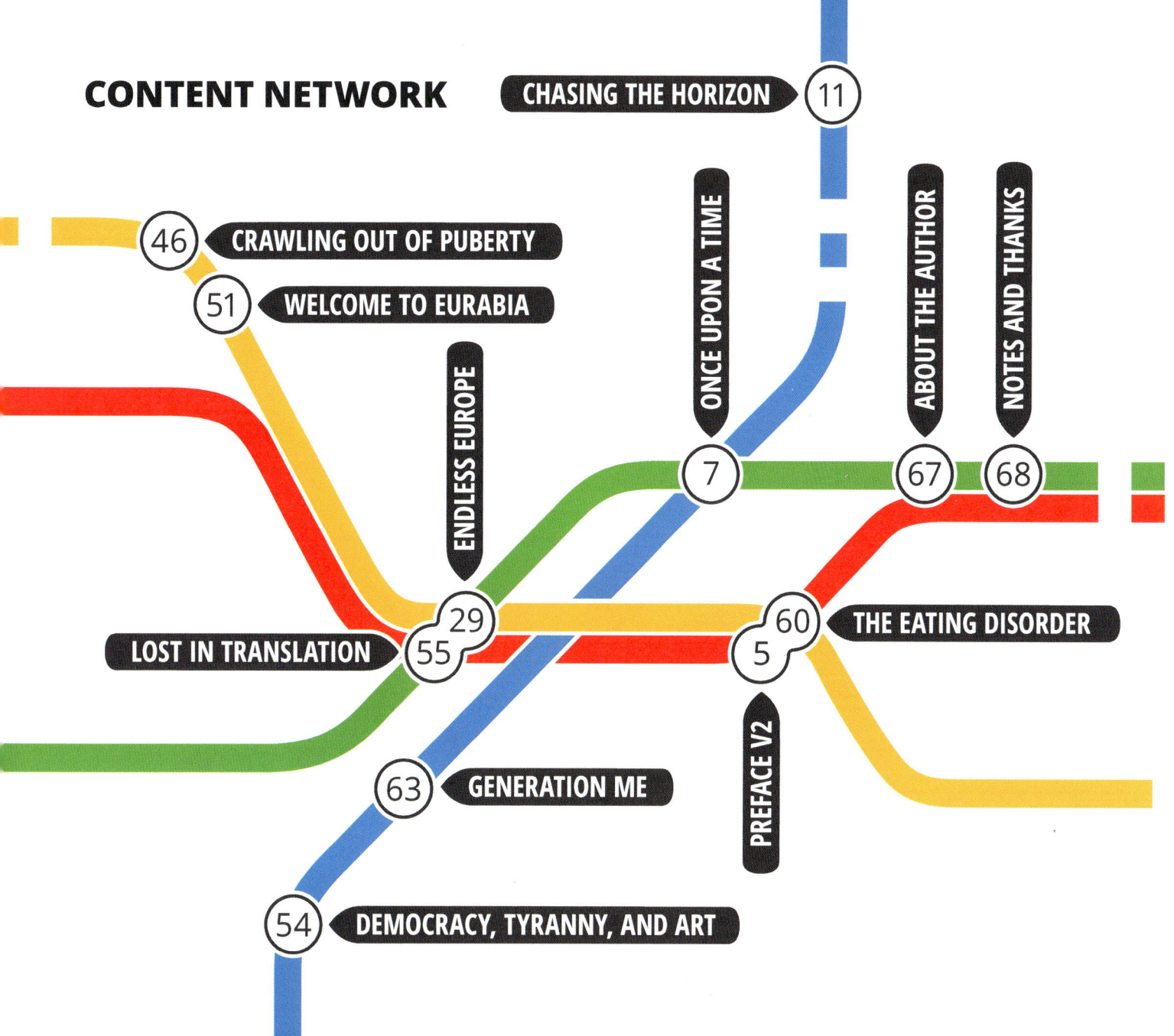

- 11 CHASING THE HORIZON
- 46 CRAWLING OUT OF PUBERTY
- 51 WELCOME TO EURABIA
- ONCE UPON A TIME
- ABOUT THE AUTHOR
- NOTES AND THANKS
- ENDLESS EUROPE
- 7
- 67
- 68
- 29
- 55 LOST IN TRANSLATION
- 60 THE EATING DISORDER
- 5 PREFACE V2
- 63 GENERATION ME
- 54 DEMOCRACY, TYRANNY, AND ART

"And I sentenced them to stay at home."

Diogenes
(after the people of Sinope sentenced him to exile)

PREFACE V2

Plenty of odd things have happened to me since I started the *Mapping Stereotypes* project, on which the *Atlas of Prejudice* is based. One of the strangest occurred last year, only a couple of weeks before the first volume of was released in Germany. I received a publishing request from Russia.

Those people must be joking, I thought. I assumed they were one of those publishers without any editorial integrity, a money laundry outlet of the legendary Russian mafia or an eccentric oligarch who didn't know what to do with his money. After all, who else would want to publish a book like mine in Russia?

There were few paragraphs inside that could have passed as mild criticism of Putin and a gay map of Europe. Western media assures us that both things are taboo behind the Velvet Curtain that separates Russia from our neatly civilized, super-democratic world.

Today, almost a year after I received this request, the Russian edition of *Atlas of Prejudice* was featured on *OTV*, the government-owned, Kremlin-backed, public television channel.

That proved two things: a) that I was a prejudiced idiot, and b) that Western propaganda overplays the censorship in the lands of the former Soviet Empire, because, at least regarding my book, I never received a single demand for a change or—to use the politically correct term—*adaptation* to specific local demand.

A month after I signed the contract with the Russian publishing house, I started negotiating with an American company, which was a subsidiary of one of the biggest publishers in the world.

After the first editorial conference, the company offered me $25,000 advance and made an interesting request:

"In the US market we feel that the cover you are using for the German (and Russian) editions is not going to resonate with potential buyers. The other issue that we are wrestling with is the title... For our market, *Atlas of Prejudice* is rather harsh sounding and does not convey the satirical aspects of your work."

I scratched my head for about a minute. Then I told them to fuck off.

After reading my answer, my agent, emotionally rock-solid as a German can be, sent me a message that contained the words "Oh my God" in it. For a fraction of a second I felt a desire to put on a police uniform and arrest myself for crimes against humanity. But after I came to my senses, I actually felt relief.

That proves two things: a) I'm still an idiot, and b) I will never be a rich author. I actually made peace with that long time ago. The only way I could end up a millionaire would be if I manage to somehow trick Google into not sending all emails coming from

Nigerian IPs directly to my spam folder. People say there's a lot of money in them.

On a less personal note, it also proves that contemporary American culture is left at the mercy of gatekeepers that tone down and tailor everything that may be hard to digest mentally, just to spit it out in the mouths of a superficial public, which is easy to tempt and manipulate.

Those gatekeepers actually want every author to believe that American people are easily scared of deep thinking, that they should be perceived as Pavlovian robots that react only under external pressure and can be trained to spend money following a pattern that is easy to analyze for the needs of those sorry human beings we call *marketing specialists*.

I would have accepted their offer if I truly believed that readers in America were as shallow as they described them. After all, taking advantage of idiots is a sin but not a deadly one. There's no "Thou shalt not sell crap to stupid Joes" commandment in the Bible. Plus, sainthood be damned, 25 grand is a lot! I have never seen so much money in my freaking life. I wish I didn't have to admit this but what the hell, if I have to go indie, let's do it all the way.

None of the Americans who saw the cover of my *Atlas of Prejudice* felt confused by it. Nobody said, "This is the next Dostoyevsky, run for your lives!"

Based on this experience I feel free to assume that my potential American readers need a nanny just as much as I need to see a naked Miley Cyrus licking a hammer. So once again on their behalf, fuck off!

Yanko Tsvetkov
November 2013, Valencia

ONCE UPON A TIME

My grandmother was born in 1932, fourteen years after the end of the First World War.

It was the year in which Aldous Huxley published the novel *Brave New World*, French president Paul Doumer got assassinated, and a mediocre Austrian painter named Adolf Hitler received German citizenship.

In the Far East Imperial Japan continued to devour parts of China, occupying Shanghai and declaring Manchuria an "independent" state. Bolivia and Paraguay started one of the bloodiest wars in South American history, fighting for control over a forsaken border region supposedly rich in oil.

In the meantime Stalin began the agricultural collectivization in the Soviet Union. It quickly led to the mass starvation of peasants known as the *Great Soviet Famine*. Germany was busy printing money faster than it was printing newspapers. Unemployment in the country reached 30%. It brought it on par with the United States, where the Dow Jones fell to its lowest level during what we now call *The Great Depression*. To add a certain twist of eccentricity to the dreadful economic climate, the first Mars chocolate bar debuted on the crisis-hit market.

But most important of all, 1932 was the year in which a feisty woman called Amelia Earhart grabbed a copy of the local newspaper in Harbour Grace, Newfoundland, got on her Lockheed Vega 5B, fired its engine, and flew over the Atlantic Ocean for 15 hours.

She eventually landed in a sloping pasture around Londonderry, Northern Ireland. Her arrival was witnessed by a local lad called Dan McCallon.

"Have you flown far?" he asked.

"From America," said Earhart and wiped the grease off her smiley face.

A battalion of world leaders hurried to congratulate *the woman of the future*, as one newspaper described her. One notable exception was Mussolini. Like all fascists, he preferred his women with an apron, bent over the oven and baking pizzas.

I'm a passionate time-traveler. It's a pleasure to explore a period when someone close to me was born. Armed with a laptop and a reliable Internet connection, I can collect enormous amounts of information. But in 1932 my grandmother's family had no clue all those things happened. Their life was simple and exclusively centered on their own immediate survival.

I am fortunate enough to remember my great-grandmother. When I was a kid she used to come and spend the winter with my grandparents. Once she told me that she never bought anything from a store.

She was exaggerating, of course. She actually did buy something from a store. It happened only once, during a trip to a nearby town. Her son was having a tantrum, pointing at a pack of biscuits, and he wouldn't stop crying. My great-grandmother must have slapped him several times, which was a universal technique for successful reasoning with spoiled children at the time. After it became apparent that it wouldn't work, she capitulated and headed for the counter.

"Every other thing I fed my children with," she said, "I produced myself, using these two hands."

Always a reluctant buyer, she was Madison Avenue's kryptonite. The carefully targeted advertising messages passed through her like neutrinos move through solid matter, leaving it completely unaffected.

Occasionally I would visit her in summer. Her village was about 100 kilometers away from my hometown. For my childhood standards, this was pretty close to the edge of the observable Universe.

I remember being bored and fascinated at the same time. It was a strange feeling. There was little I could do in a place with less than 100 houses. In the early 1980s the urbanization had already emptied most of the agrarian villages, leaving only old people behind. Without much hesitation, their children traded the comfort of the family nest for the exciting opportunities of the big city.

There was a huge oil refinery nearby. You could see its enormous chimneys from kilometers away. The large factories pumping smoke into the atmosphere were treated as sacred temples by the communist state. We even had them on our banknotes.

The refinery was undeniably a fascinating sight, especially at night when you could see the tips of its chimneys burning brightly. The emissions made the entire region smell of rotten eggs. Every time we passed by I used to vomit a little bit. On the other side of the village there was another miracle of communist progress—a military airbase. The jets often flew over my great-grandmother's house with pompous supersonic roar, ready to deflect any imperialist attack on our precious oil refinery.

The house had one characteristic that genuinely scared me: the outside toilet. When I wanted to pee I had to actually go out. It just didn't make sense. Surely the people who built this house were very stupid, I thought. Later I realized the village had no sewage system. When my grandmother was born they didn't even have electricity.

My grandmother's life was rarely affected by any events that took place beyond the horizon. When I asked her if she remembered World War II she said that she knew about it but it didn't directly influence her life.

Part of the reason of her blissful unawareness was that no major military battles took place in Bulgaria. For her, World War II resembled one of those stereotypical pre-Napoleonic European wars in which small armies clashed occasionally, diplomats exchanged notes, royal relatives traded virgins and at the end everybody settled for a compromise. Most common people barely noticed any difference.

In such a world any thought about globalization was as abstract a Kandinsky painting. There were few reasons to be worried about things that happened in a neighboring country, let alone in one across the ocean. All news reports were local and delivered by an authority that people trusted almost explicitly. Skepticism was usually a bourgeois luxury unknown to peasants.

Because of this, my grandmother still has difficulties sorting out real problems from biased meaningless filler when she watches the news. According to her everything contained in a news report is—by definition—true and equally important.

She has no idea that news reports are created by people like her and thus can often be incredibly subjective. She imagines them growing on trees in the great cosmic ether, where hardworking journalists come once a day to pick those ripe enough for mass consumption.

The constant flow of information makes her extremely neurotic. She tries to remember every detail

THE WORLD ACCORDING TO MY GRANDMOTHER 1932

- Shepherd's Bush Road
- Cowherd's Boulevard
- A Less Muddy Street
- **Grandmotherville** Population ±100
- Me!
- Gossip Hill
- THE WHEAT FIELD
- RABBITS
- MICE
- My Aunt's Street
- End of the World
- My Uncle's Street
- Wild Bore Boulevard
- My Cousin's Street
- THE SCARY FOREST
- COMMUNISTS
- MONSTERS
- THE WATERMELON FIELD

she hears, and when she inevitably fails, she blames it on her fading memory.

"There was an essay test today in the schools but I forgot its theme," she once complained to me, "I even wrote it down, so I wouldn't forget it. But I lost the note!"

"But grandma! Who cares? Why would you want to remember such things in the first place?"

"Well," she said, "I wouldn't have to remember it if I managed not to lose the note on which I wrote it down."

She perceives the mass media as an institution, not as a communication tool. There are still traces of this attitude left among the older generations in many industrialized countries. Those people often feel disillusioned by the contemporary world. Their nostalgic memories about the good old days tempt them to see apocalypses in trends that are simply adaptations to new conditions, the nature of which they cannot grasp.

There have always been cultural and technological shifts from generation to generation but their dynamism has rarely been so hectic. The shift today is truly profound and its influence over the media is only a side effect of the enormous change in the way we exchange information.

Many of us still remember the time in which access to knowledge meant access to a library and all the bureaucracy that came with it. The number of books we possessed was often used as a measure of our intelligence. Those ideas are so ancient that, as ages passed by, they turned from practical concepts into universal principles without which advanced civilizations are considered impossible.

The first library known to historians existed in the temple of Nippur, around 2500 B.C. It kept the oldest written record about the universal pool party that the Bible would later call *The Great Flood*. We also know that private non-religious libraries existed at least since the Classical period in Ancient Greece, of which the Royal Library of Alexandria is the most famous example.

Ever since the priests of Nippur started keeping score of the amount of grain donated to their god Enlil, information needed a designated physical space in order to be stored reliably. For 4500 years those needs were perfectly met by buildings strong enough to withstand the menacing natural disasters and the much more destructive political cataclysms.

The people who didn't have constant access to those buildings but nevertheless wanted to keep information handy, had to memorize everything and carry it in their heads. Such an "agricultural" approach to knowledge was incredibly effective for ages until in the last few centuries the amount of our collectively accumulated wisdom drastically exceeded the capacity of the single human brain.

It will be incredibly naïve to imagine that we can continue to pile up our knowledge in such "granaries". Today storage devices are incredibly cheap, easy to carry around, and almost everybody can afford a basic Internet connection. This means that someone living in Europe doesn't need to book a transatlantic flight to access to the US Library of Congress.

I wonder if Amelia Earhart imagined such a thing would be possible when she flew over the ocean in 1932. I certainly couldn't picture it as a child and even science fiction authors rarely envisioned something like the Internet.

To paraphrase the third law of Arthur Clarke—for my grandmother this technology is indistinguishable from magic. When I look at the world through her eyes, I feel enormously privileged to be alive at the start of such an enormous shift in human history.

CHASING THE HORIZON

1492 was a blockbuster year in world history with a beginning worthy of a Venezuelan soap opera.

There was barely any time for opening credits. On the second day of January the last Muslim state on the Iberian Peninsula, the Emirate of Granada, was finally conquered by the armies of the Catholic Monarchs, a fanatical incestuous couple comprising of Isabella I, Queen of Castile, and Ferdinand II, King of Aragon. Their personal union would later become the foundation of what we know today as Spain.

For those lucky enough to be there, the sight of the surrender must have felt like the ultimate Castilian wet dream. The cross of Christ hung on the walls of the enchanting Alhambra palace. The Moorish Emir Muhammad XII slowly approached, holding the keys of his city, ready to present them to his conquerors and kiss their hands as a sign of capitulation.

Suddenly, there came a dramatic ceremonial twist. To save the dignity of her son from complete emasculation, Muhammad's mother begged the Catholic Monarchs to amend the protocol, so the city can pass in their possession without the aforementioned humiliating kiss. Isabella and Ferdinand agreed.

The crowd, deeply moved by the merciful gesture, spontaneously started to sing the Catholic evergreen *Te Deum* and burst into tears of joy. Rumor has it that only the mercy of the almighty Christian God, who opened the heavens to take a peek at the momentous celebration, spared those people from severe dehydration by miraculously reinforcing their lacrimal glands with holy water.

According to a popular legend, when Muhammad XII reached a nearby hill on his way to exile, he turned back to see his beloved palace for the last time. Overtaken by sadness and corroding sense of loss, he started to weep until his mother, a true incarnation of a perfect Muslim dominatrix, consoled him with the words, "Thou dost weep like a woman for what thou couldst not defend as a man."

Among the exalted crowd of Christians, who celebrated the fall of the Muslim Emirate, was a Genovese sailor called Christopher Columbus. He had more than one reason to be happy. The Catholic Monarchs had promised to finance his voyage to discover a Western route to India, one that would be free from the interference of infidels like Muhammad

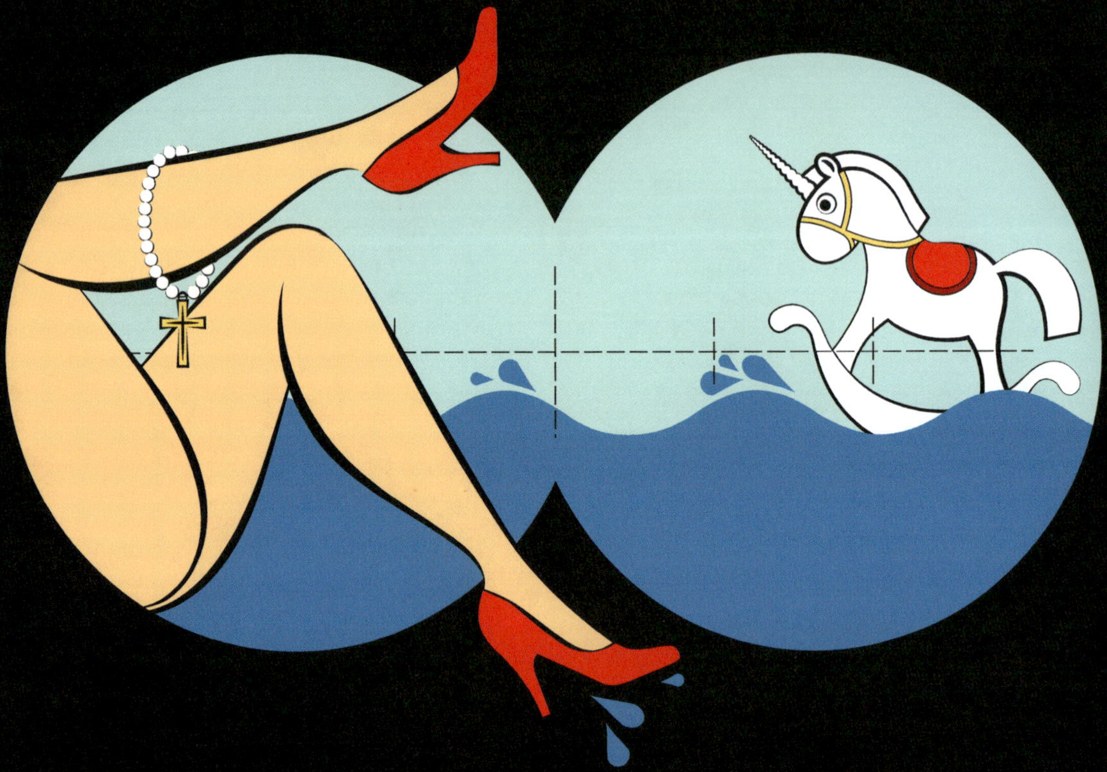

XII and his much more powerful brother-in-faith, the Ottoman Sultan in Constantinople.

Most people believed Columbus was either on drugs or simply delusional. Yet Isabella and Ferdinand had little to lose from subsidizing a suicide mission of three ships. However, if such a route truly existed, Castile would have a chance to surpass both the incredibly wealthy Ottoman Empire to the East and the increasingly ambitious Portuguese Kingdom to the West, which was stubbornly looking for an Eastern maritime route to India.

In our age of reason we are often tempted to imagine Columbus as an adventurous explorer driven by an insatiable curiosity and a passion for the unknown.

The truth is a little bit different. Europe was a messy place at the end of the 15th Century. A significant part of it was ruled by Muslims. The Spanish Reconquista may have pushed out the Moors to Africa and brought Christianity back to the Iberian Peninsula after 700 years of struggle but in the East another great Muslim power was rapidly chipping away land from the Danubian Christian kingdoms. Its ambitions were far bigger than those of the small Moorish states in the dysfunctional Al Andalus, whose last remnant was the decadent and defenseless Emirate of Granada.

The Ottomans wanted it all and they wanted it now. After the conquest of Constantinople, they laid claim to the entire region previously ruled by the Roman Empire, which is to say no less than half of the continent.

European history is incredibly poor in symbols. Usually one would expect that as ages pass by, new ideas would come and older ones would be forgotten. Instead, many of them were repeatedly recycled, like a plot of a profitable action movie.

One of the ever recurring obsessions of various European rulers was the restoration of the Roman Empire. The city of Rome was considered the political center of the European world for so long that it became a synonym of political power. This didn't change when Emperor Constantine abruptly moved the Roman capital to Constantinople. True to their habit, people just started referring to the new capital as the Second Rome.

In 476, after centuries of military struggle, moral decay, and political bankruptcy, the First Rome, or whatever ruins remained of it, finally fell in the arms of the barbarians. Despite no longer being in possession of its ancient capital, the Roman Empire continued to thrive to the East as if nothing significant happened.

The Romans in Constantinople could have never imagined that in the 16th Century a German historian called Hieronymus Wolf would coin a new name for their state—*Byzantine Empire*. From a historical point of view this made as little sense as naming modern Iraq *Babylonia*. But Western historians gradually fell in love with it, probably because it mischievously implied that the empire ruled from Constantinople had nothing to do with Rome itself.

For all intents and purposes (and historical accuracy), the Byzantine Empire was a direct continuation of its ancient predecessor. Despite the fact that Greek relatively quickly replaced Latin as the main language, people there continued to refer to themselves and their state as Roman.

The name change in the West served to historically legitimize the Frankenstein monster called Holy Roman Empire, which was inhabited exclusively by sinners and never had Rome as its capital.

The Papacy started the Holy Roman Empire project as an attempt to maintain its spiritual and political independence, a frivolity that the Byzantine emperors and their subordinate patriarchs in the East had no desire to tolerate.

In order to solve this problem once and for all, Pope Leo III came up with a brilliant idea. He seduced the most powerful leader in the West, Charlemagne, and crowned him a Roman Emperor on

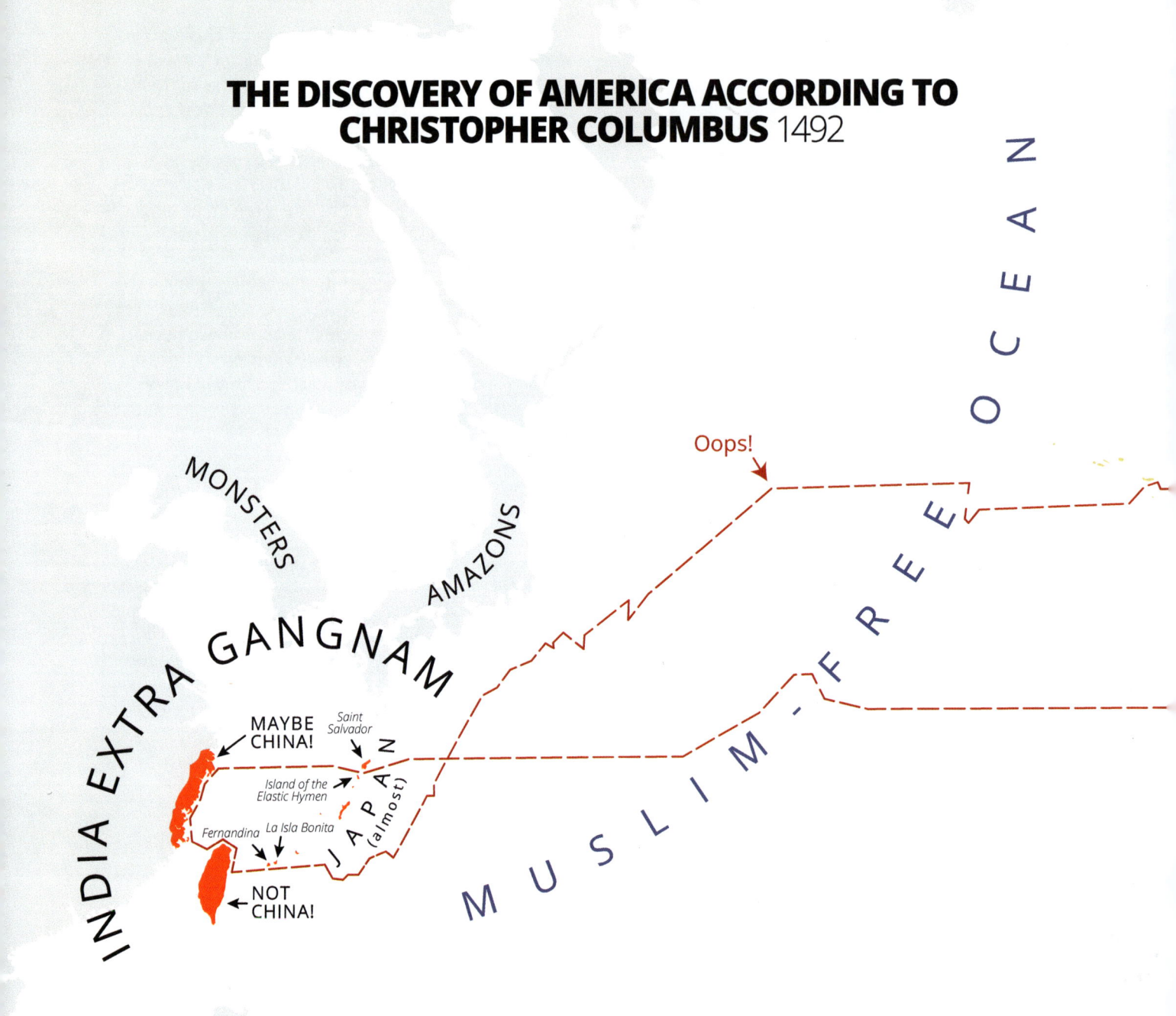

THE DISCOVERY OF AMERICA ACCORDING TO CHRISTOPHER COLUMBUS 1492

MUSLIM-FREE OCEAN

Oops!

MONSTERS

AMAZONS

INDIA EXTRA GANGNAM

MAYBE CHINA!

Saint Salvador

Island of the Elastic Hymen

Fernandina La Isla Bonita

JAPAN (almost)

NOT CHINA!

UNICORNS
PARSNIPS
SOAP OPERAS
DRAGONS
JEWISH GHETTO
UNHOLY MESS
FAKE CATHOLICS
BANKRUPT RENAISSANCE
HEAD START BAY
ENVIOUS SNOBS
INFECTED AREA
IDIOTS
TRUE CATHOLICS
Fuck Yeah!
TOMATO-FREE SEA
MOORISH SPA & SUMMER RETREAT
McMUMMY®
SATAN
AFRICAN AMERICANS

Christmas day, exactly 800 years after the (alleged) birth of Jesus.

Both men yearned for each other like a desert yearns for rain. Charlemagne, as vein as a Hollywood actress, was eager to consolidate his conquests in Italy and Saxony. Leo III needed an ally with a sizable army to cushion the Papacy from the Byzantine interference and extend his ambitions for universal spiritual domination.

It can be speculated who was the real beneficiary of this arranged marriage. Charlemagne probably cared more about slaying insubordinate Saxons, who just happened to be non-Christian, than about the holiness of his title. Leo III must have considered politics a necessary evil that could be tolerated until the second coming of his beloved employer Jesus Christ.

However, 1200 years later, the Papacy still stands, stubbornly holding on to the past, and preaching about the dangers of condoms and genetic engineering. Charlemagne's Empire disintegrated soon after his death, and all that remains from it today, is the emperor's grave in the famous Aachen Cathedral, which, quite ironically, is owned by the Catholic Church. The spirit must be truly mightier than the sword.

Once they tasted the sweet nectar of world domination, the Roman popes never gave up their right to legitimize every political ruler in the world. It may seem naïve and delusional in retrospective but those people weren't at all detached from reality. They simply realized it can be bent upon their will.

Just in case someone had doubts about the seriousness of their claims, the popes started wearing a fancy 3-layer tiara that looked like a late 20th Century beauty parlor hair-dryer. Extravagant clothing has always been used for intimidation purposes but the papal tiara was a true masterpiece of its kind. It was also uncomfortable to wear, although what is a neck injury next to the promise of universal supremacy?

When the Ottomans captured Constantinople in 1453 they didn't simply conquer a city. They acquired a symbol. It immediately became the capital of their empire and the 21-year-old Sultan Mehmed II titled himself *Kayser-i Rûm*, which translated from Turkish meant *Roman Caesar*. Thus, according to Mehmed's logic, he obtained the right to rule over the First Rome as well.

The Ottomans never managed to conquer Italy, even though in 1480 they occupied Otranto, a city in Apulia, which at the time was part of the Neapolitan Kingdom, the southern neighbor of the Papal State.

Sixtus IV, who had the misfortune to reign as Pope in those troubled times, got truly scared and even started making plans for Rome's evacuation, in case the Ottoman hordes from Otranto decided to head north. Drawing fire exit labels with one hand and calling for a global Christian crusade against the infidels with the other, he finally hit the jackpot when Mehmed II died and a dynastic battle prevented further Ottoman expansion.

Perhaps this little twist of fate saved the Roman Pantheon from becoming a mosque and ensured that the just painted nude bodies of Adam and God in the Sistine chapel would not be covered by layers of hypnotizing arabesques. In stark contrast to the Papacy, the Muslims hadn't yet developed an appreciation for homoerotic pornography.

The Roman claims of the Ottoman sultans were never truly relinquished. A testament to their ambition is the fact that the official name of their capital remained Constantinople throughout the entire history of their empire. It was changed to Istanbul only after the last Ottoman dynasty was removed from power and Turkey became a republic.

Another, far more interesting testament, is an engraving by Agostino Veneziano with the portrait of Suleiman the Magnificent, the great-grandson of Mehmed II. On it, the Sultan is depicted wearing a 4-layer tiara, especially handcrafted for him in Venice, the fashion capital of the Renaissance.

Its top is adorned with a huge feather, a provocation every Italian would no doubt appreciate. Nobody

EUROPE ACCORDING TO BAYEZID II 1500

- HERE BE GENIES
- FUNNY PEOPLE
- ALUM ADDICTS
- IN VITRO ARISTOCRACY CLINIC
- FANATICS ON STEROIDS
- MEGALOMANIAC
- YUMMY!
- TAMED VAMPIRES
- COUSINS
- IBLIS
- ARMPIT LICE
- CHEATERS!
- EVA & ADOLF
- Auschwitz
- MY ROMAN SELF
- SHIA PEST
- PUBIC LICE
- THE WET SILK ROAD
- OH LOOK, INDIA! (Just Kidding!)

knows whether the Pope received a signed copy of the portrait, but Suleiman never missed an opportunity to show the tiara to his ambassadors. As diplomatic common sense dictates, if you can't conquer your enemies, you can at least tease them!

Ottoman Constantinople, for its part, became an obsession of another rising superpower to the north, Russia, whose capital was often referred to as the Third Rome after the Ottomans conquered the Second.

No longer a physical location but an abstract cause, Rome became the European Apple of Discord just like Abraham became the common founder of three monotheistic religions that continue to despise each other.

It may sound counterintuitive but shared symbols don't always bring people closer. Very often they have the opposite effect and, instead of love and understanding, provoke hatred and envy.

It was such envy that inspired Christian Europe in the 15th Century to emancipate itself from the much more advanced Muslim powers of the East. The Ottomans and the Arabs controlled trade with India through the Red Sea and the famous Silk Road, another important symbol in European history. Being constantly at war with the Muslim world, Christian Europe had little chance to negotiate favorable prices for all the exotic goods it was craving.

The solution was easier to formulate than to execute. Europeans had to find a way to trade directly with India just like their Roman predecessors did for centuries.

It's definitely not true that at the time people believed the Earth was flat and Columbus had to convince everybody of the opposite. In fact, people were well aware of the roundness of the planet at least since Aristotle found a way to prove it in 330 BC.

Some historians claim the misconception of the flat Earth belief was intentionally spread during the 19th Century by the early supporters of the theory of evolution who wanted to portray the Catholic Church as more backward than it actually was. But neither the Church nor any educated scholar of the Columbian era insisted that the Earth was a giant pancake carried by elephants. Ironically, such ludicrous beliefs would develop much later in human history, proving beyond doubt that there's not a direct correlation between scientific progress and human stupidity.

What people in the 15th Century didn't know for sure was whether Africa could be circumnavigated. Until then nobody bothered to check because it wasn't a necessity. Most thinkers were satisfied to simply theorize about it.

Some believed Africa extended so far to the south that its landmass encircled the Indian Ocean and met with Asia at its other end, making India inaccessible to any ships from the Atlantic Ocean.

Others believed the Earth was divided in climatic zones that prevented anyone from crossing the Equator. According to this theory, the sun rays at the equatorial zone were so powerful that they made the seawater boil. A voyage through this region would turn every ship into a steaming soup of human flesh and crackling wood.

There were navigational challenges as well. Sea travel was mainly done along the coasts. No one dared to head for open sea. The compass was a relatively new invention, and Europeans were too reliant on the constellations of the Northern Hemisphere for orientation.

But things were starting to change and when Columbus entered the scene, the Iberian kingdoms were building the most advanced ships in Europe.

What didn't change was the scope of people's imagination. The same old stories about gold and spices ignited the same old ambitions. Layer after layer of myths, from Alexander the Great to Marco Polo, pointed at India as the source of all riches.

Occasionally there was a tale or two about people who headed west for something slightly different. Saint Brendan of Clonfert departed from his native Ireland in search of the Island of the Blessed. He was

News Feed		2
Paintings		
Close Friends		12
Harem		1 204

PAGES
Twerking Slavic Girls
Say No To Booze!
I "Heart" Vienna!
Muslim Pride '29
Ottoman Idol

INTERESTS
Poetry
Tulips
Head Gear

Suleiman the Magnificent, Roman Emperor

Went for a stroll around the Venetian market the other day and saw this hat. Could NOT resist! OMG, fabulous! Is it not, Pope Clement VII?

Like · Comment · Share

♥ 10 people like this.   Top Comments ▼

3 shares

Pope Clement VII Are helmets still mandatory in Constantinople, my dear?
Like · Reply · 37 minutes ago

Suleiman the Magnificent, Roman Emperor Only if you drive a Vespa, darling! <3
Like · 20 minutes ago

Francis I of France Looking GOOOOD! Kisses! Muah muah muah!!! <3
Like · Reply · 20 minutes ago

Charles V Holy Roman Emperor Sad to see people today so obsessed with the way they look. :((((
Like · Reply · 32 minutes ago

SPONSORED ADS

Finest Iberian Ham
porkofspain.com
The finest pigs slain by freshly converted Christians!

McBratwurst
wurstunddrang.de
Embrace phallic food! Say no to döners this Christmas!

one of those monks that felt compelled to spread Christianity as far as possible. Before embarking on his great adventure, Brendan circumnavigated Ireland to make sure that each and every person he encountered was truly convinced that a virgin woman could get pregnant, and her hymen could be restored after the birth of her child. Only then could he allow himself to head west.

On his journey he encountered a lot of interesting things that totally made sense: a coagulated sea, devils, Judas vacationing in Iceland, lots of sheep, and several birds singing Christian psalms. In the meantime, a monster attacked his ship but God, as always interested in the smallest details of human affairs, tweaked the laws of gravity, so the waters of the sea could shift and save Brendan from peril.

That's right! Whenever they didn't dream of gold and spices, Europeans yearned to baptize the entire world, just in case there was any doubt that their God was the True One.

The thrill of exploring the unknown, of solving the mysteries that lie beyond someone's personal imagination, wasn't on the menu yet. It had to wait a few centuries until the Age of Enlightenment, which succeeded the creative chaos of what we now affectionately call Renaissance, began to transform European civilization, and from a tribe of proselytizing bigots turned it into true citizens of the world. The process is still continuing today.

Columbus unintentionally started the trend on October 12, 1492 when he set foot on an island in what is today the Bahama Archipelago. Just like Cervantes never revealed the hometown of Don Quixote, Columbus wasn't very precise in describing which island exactly had the honor to welcome the first Castilians to the New World.

Moreover, there are different versions about what he thought he discovered. According to some sources Columbus was convinced he had reached Japan, which Westerners at the time called *Cipango*. According to others, he thought he arrived in India. Nobody could make a real difference anyway. For the Europeans, every piece of land east of the Ganges River was pure myth. They called those regions *India extra Gangem*.

Historians agree about one important thing. Columbus had no idea he landed on a new continent. He remained convinced that he had found a route to India until his death. It would take some time for Europeans to actually *discover* that he discovered a continent.

There is a Slavic proverb saying that everything new is just well-forgotten old stuff. It's probably not a secret to anybody today that Columbus wasn't the first European to reach the New World.

To begin with, the boundary between the Old and the New World was purely subjective, drawn by the ignorance and the technological limitations of Christian Europe. But during the blissful stagnation of the Early Middle Ages there was another kind of Europe to the North. It belonged to the Vikings. They were often described as bloodthirsty animals by the medieval Christian historians, who just like the Ancient Greeks, had the habit to consider every pagan civilization inherently barbaric.

A lot of time had to pass until Christian Europe started to study Viking history without dogmatic prejudice. This didn't prevent the Vikings from exploring the entire European continent, reaching as far south as African Morocco and Asian Anatolia.

However, their real geographical achievements were to the northwest of Scandinavia. By the year 825 they reached the Faroe Islands and in 874 they arrived in Iceland, where they settled and would later write down their legends, known today as the *Icelandic sagas*.

Those stories started a solid literary tradition which is still alive today. "Ad ganga med bok I maganum" is a popular saying in Iceland. It means "everyone gives birth to a book". It's almost literally true. One in ten inhabitants of this small rocky island is a published author.

EUROPE ACCORDING TO THE VIKINGS 1000

In 982, less than a century after their arrival in Iceland, the Vikings reached Greenland. In 1000 they went even further and landed in Newfoundland, where they settled comfortably in a place called *Vinland*. The first known American with European parents was born soon after. His name was Snorri Thorfinnsson.

Of course, according to modern geographic convention, this is not entirely true because Greenland also belongs to America, and Vinland was settled 18 years later. That's enough time for a Greenlandic baby to steal the coveted title.

The problem is that Greenland has always been politically considered part of Europe, which makes things extremely confusing. After the mapping of the tectonic plates in the early 20th Century, definitions became even more elusive. When people started following the plate boundaries, it became clear that half of Iceland and Eastern Siberia should also be considered American.

How can we then speak of continental discoveries and why should we care that a xenophobic Christian fanatic like Christopher Columbus reached the Americas in 1492?

Well, whatever discoveries were made by the Vikings, it's an undeniable fact that few of the pious Christian Europeans from the South had a clue what was going on in the cold recesses of the barren Arctic. The Vikings were the only ones to benefit from their own discoveries. After their civilization declined, their adventures were either forgotten or turned into myths. The only memories left alive were those of plunder and rape.

Another thing that was conveniently forgotten was the booming trade between the Southerners and the "savages" from the North. Naturally, the Christians considered trade with the Vikings and the Muslims deeply immoral, but in reality they could rarely resist the temptation of the exotic goods those infidels had to offer.

The epic love triangle of early medieval trade stretched from China to the shores of Iceland and the ports of the Italian maritime republics. Textile, spices, gem stones, and fur were transported on Persian caravans, Viking ships, and Frankish mules.

The infidels had a taste for pranks. The Vikings, who were hunting for narwhals in the cold Arctic waters, sold their tusks to the superstitious European nobility, advertising them as unicorn horns. Demand was high because the naïve Southerners were convinced beyond doubt that unicorns truly existed. Not that anybody had seen one. People just yearned to believe in made-up stories.

The highly intellectual Leonardo da Vinci describes the unicorn hunt as a cunning ritual with disturbingly sexual undertones:

"The unicorn, through its intemperance and not knowing how to control itself, for the love it bears to fair maidens forgets its ferocity and wildness; and laying aside all fear it will go up to a seated damsel and go to sleep in her lap, and thus the hunters take it."

After reading lines like these, one can honestly regret that Sigmund Freud wasn't born during the Renaissance. But I wouldn't be surprised if someone finds an old book somewhere in Iceland titled *Saga of the Sexually Repressed Southerner Who Traded Gold for Whale Teeth*.

The stubborn belief in unicorns continued to thrive long after the last Viking embraced the Bible. Finally, in 1638, a physician from Denmark called Ole Worm, who became famous for his studies in embryology, proved beyond doubt that the unicorn horns on the market were actually narwhal tusks. It took some time for the evidence to sink in. Powdered unicorn horns continued to be sold as medicine at least for another century.

But the real prank-masters were the Muslims. They never missed an opportunity to make their hypochondriac Christian neighbors to the west look stu-

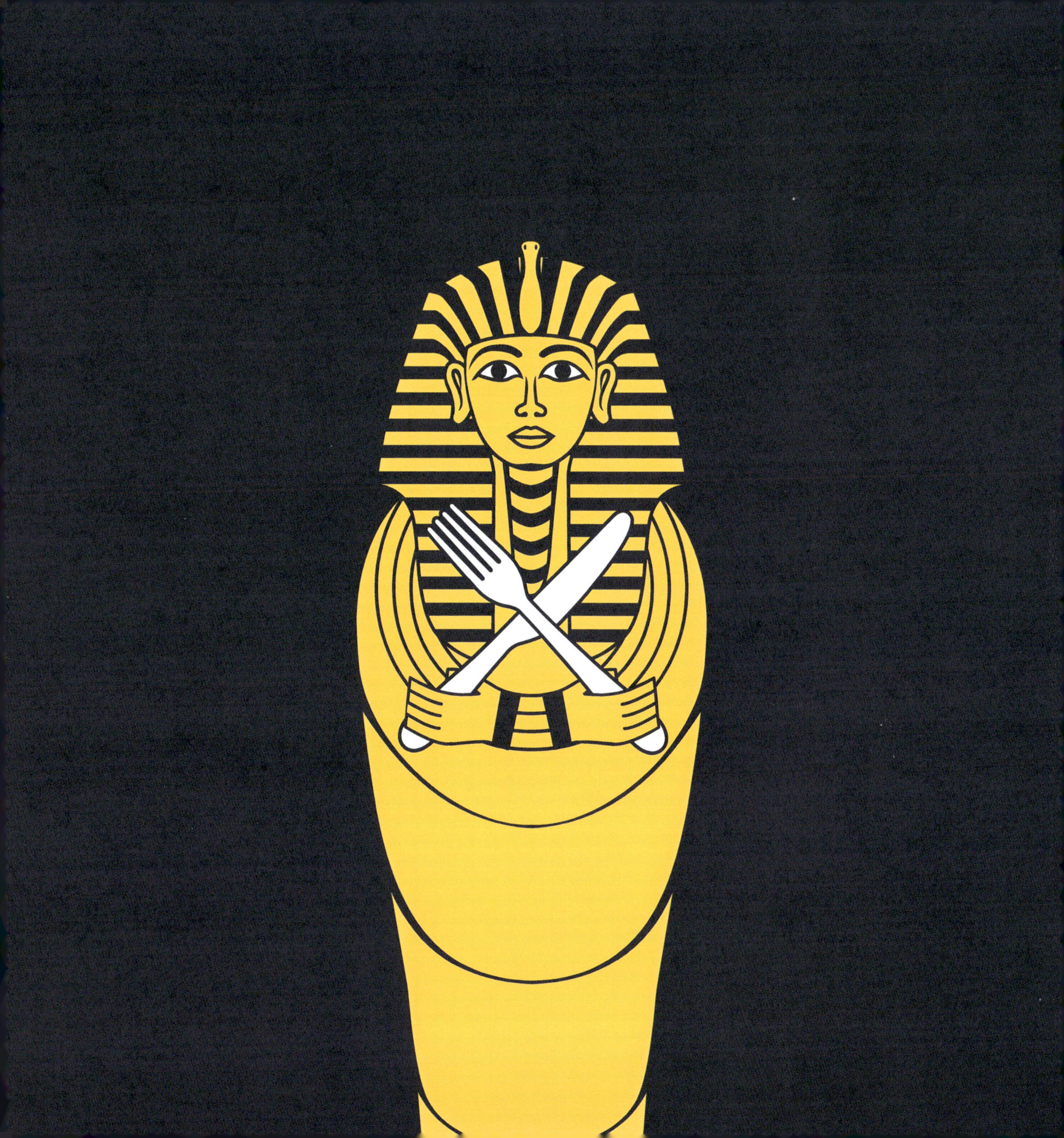

pid. After years of selling overpriced aphrodisiacs like black pepper, they found a true soft spot. Mummies.

Mummies weren't always rare. In fact they were quite abundant until at least the 16th Century. Then, for the weirdest of reasons, the extremely civilized Europeans started eating them.

Ironically, this happened around the time in which the tomato arrived to Europe from America. It took about two centuries for it to appear as an ingredient in a European recipe because people feared it was toxic. The mummy, on the other hand, was an instant success.

Thomas Joseph Pettigrew, a famous surgeon, who entertained bored British aristocrats by performing autopsies on mummies and even mummified the body of Alexander, the 10th Duke of Hamilton, wrote in his *History of Egyptian Mummies*:

"No sooner was it credited that mummy constituted an article of value in the practice of medicine than many speculators embarked in the trade; the tombs were sacked, and as many mummies as could be obtained were broken into pieces for the purpose of sale"

The craze took Europe by storm, and ground mummy became as widely used as aspirin is today, at least among the people who could afford to pay for it. Francois I, the king of France himself, considered it a wonder medicine and always carried a pouch on his neck for emergencies. Similar to the unicorn horn, mummy remedies were prescribed long after it became apparent that they were neither medicines nor safe to consume.

If you think this wasn't gruesome enough, there's an even more sinister twist to the story. After Europeans ate the main supply, and it became harder and harder to harvest mummies from the ancient Egyptian graves, some traders started producing fake ones by soaking dead human bodies in bitumen. Strangely, it was bitumen itself that initially sparked the belief in the healing powers of Egyptian mummies, whose color and texture resembled the mysterious substance, which was a rarity in Europe ever since ancient times. Pliny the Elder prescribed bitumen for toothache.

History is full with such absurdities. They seem obviously ridiculous to the educated modern mind, but our forefathers didn't live in a world mapped by satellites. Despite the efforts of many reckless men who attempted to establish global civilizations, the Antiquity and the Middle Ages were times of ever present mystery and uncertainty. Cyrus II, Alexander, Trajan, and Genghis Khan pushed the boundaries of the known world farther and farther, but until the Age of Discovery no single civilization ever succeeded to explore the entire planet and gather the vast amounts of knowledge we are now being served on a plate and fed with a silver spoon.

In the pre-Columbian days people must have stared at the horizon with the same sense of wonder with which we look at the vastness of interstellar space.

It took more than a year for the top scientists at NASA to determine whether Voyager I, the first man-made object to ever leave the Solar System, had truly moved beyond the Heliopause, the boundary after which the Sun's influence stops, and interstellar space begins. Now we know that the probe passed this elusive region on August 25, 2012 and we all missed the opportunity to pop a bottle of champagne.

Perhaps after a couple of centuries, if we survive that long, people would celebrate Voyager Day instead of Columbus Day.

There's little doubt that most of our assumptions about the Universe will be either corrected or proven wrong. Our children will probably giggle at the ridiculousness of those refuted ideas. No matter how knowledgeable modern physicists would like to appear, we are still gambling with concepts like string theory, dark matter, parallel universes, and super-symmetry. We even build enormous expensive laboratories like CERN, just to be able to smash electrons and search for mysterious new particles among their debris.

DEEP SPACE EXPLORATION 2013

4¼
light years

Distance to the nearest star

THE SUN — HIC SVNT DRACONES — PROXIMA CENTAURI

17
light hours

Distance traveled by Voyager I

The real importance of the great Age of Exploration and its culmination with the first voyage of Columbus, is that it kick-started globalization, and ultimately pushed the mythical boundaries of our world to outer space.

People who study the legacy of Columbus may argue about the goals and the methods he employed, they may criticize his cruelty, which led to his incarceration and stripped him of his governorship of the West Indies. It was an age equally rich in heroism and disgrace, in spiritual conquest and moral defeat.

A heartbreakingly enormous part of the Native American population was exterminated by systematic genocide or by European diseases brought by the same ships that helped expand trade and facilitate the routes for future cultural exchange.

The spoils of the Spanish conquest were irresponsibly wasted in fanatic religious wars across Europe, in which the German states in Central Europe lost more than 30% of their own population. This gruesome fact is rarely mentioned by historians when they discuss the detrimental effects of the plunder of the New World.

One can speculate that this tragedy delayed the development and emancipation of Germany with at least a century. It left the embryonic nation to rot under its own provincialism. As a result of this, Germany's grotesquely delayed monster-birth completely destroyed what was left of the European balance of power and paved the way for WWI, at the beginning of which Spain was already a political corpse with zero value to any international alliance.

Karma has a twisted sense of humor but even that cannot diminish the importance of this first voyage in the belly of the Atlantic and the reckless ambition of the sailor who initiated it.

Columbus was a man living in an age when, for the first time in written human history, a civilization acquired both the resources and the technology to truly connect all parts of the surface of our planet, no matter how remote or mystical they might have been for previous generations. Just like Voyager is not a product of a single team of American scientists, the expedition of Columbus employed the efforts, the knowledge, and occasionally, the ignorance of all civilizations that preceded it.

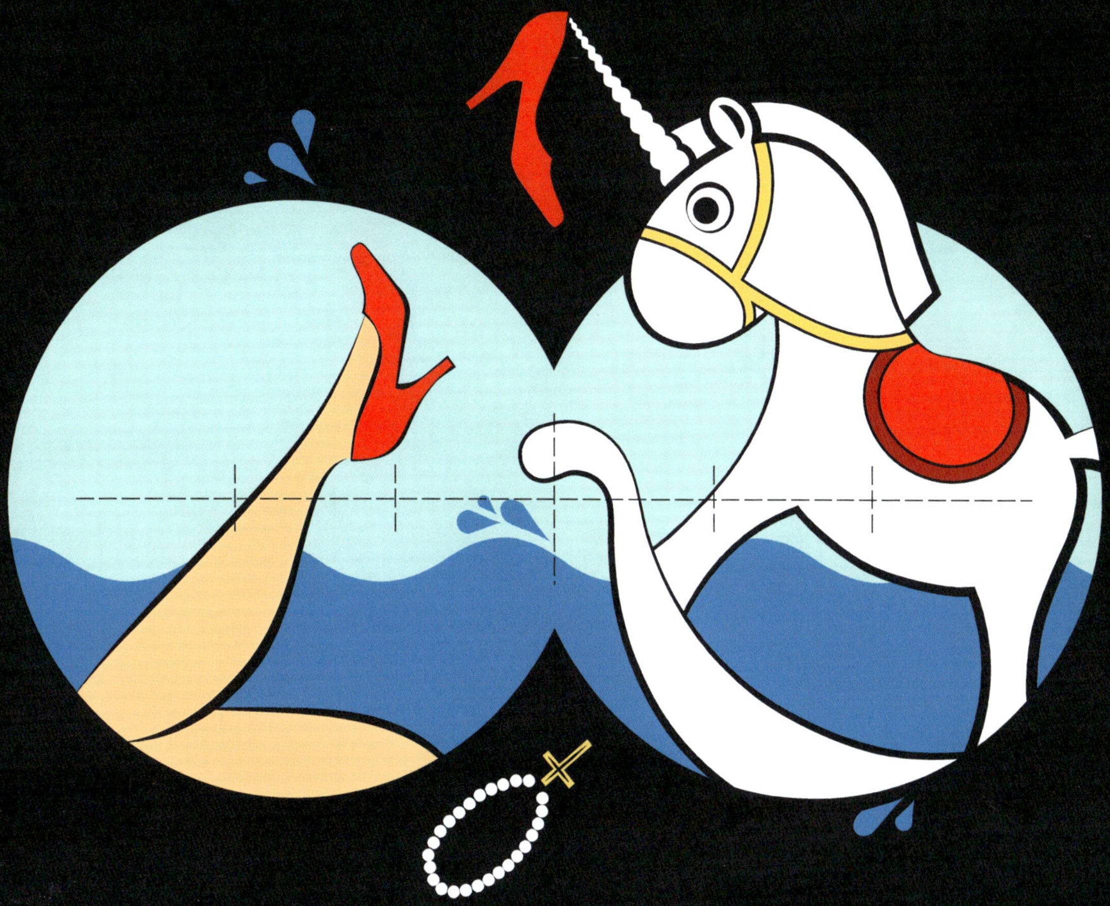

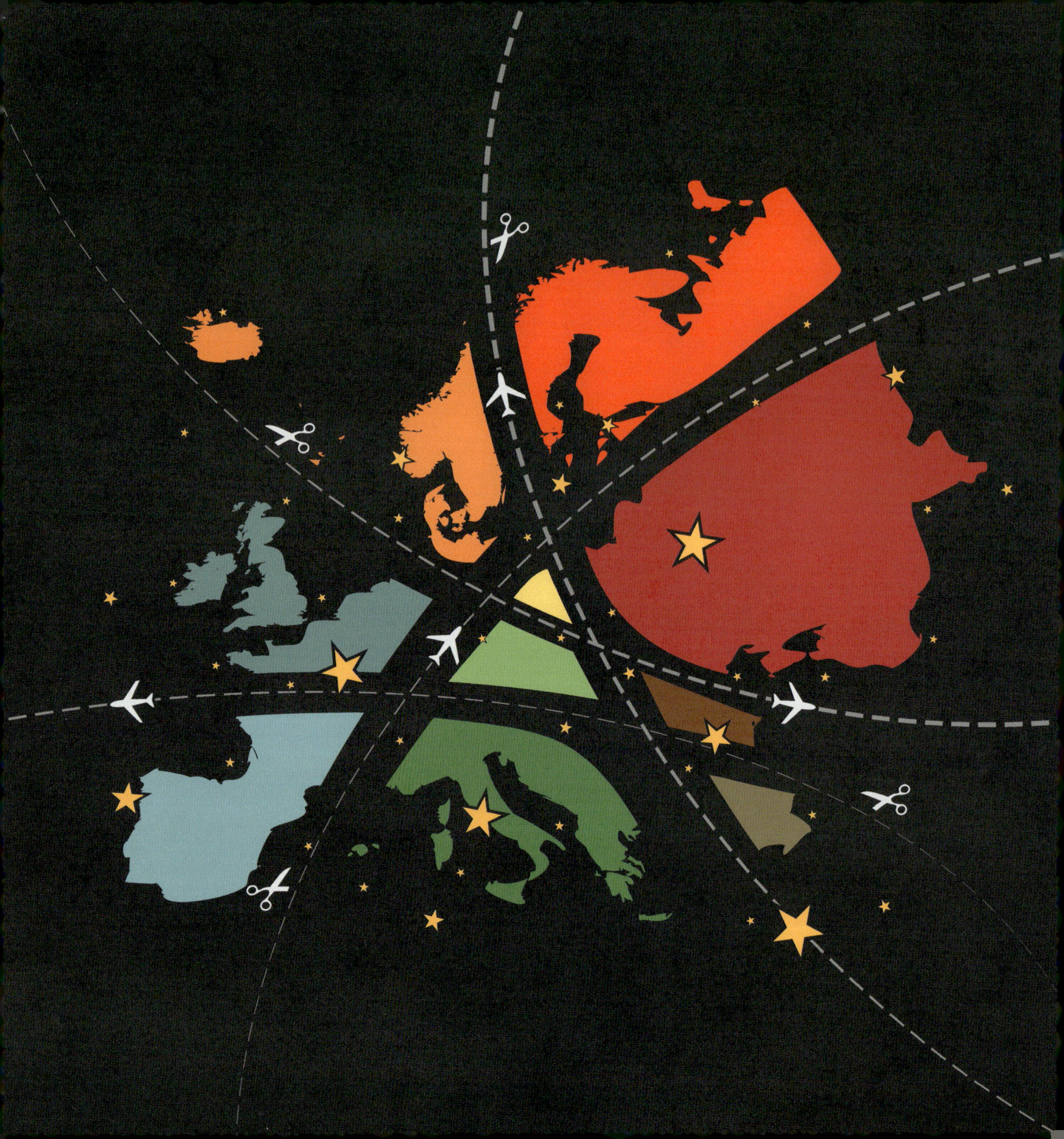

ENDLESS EUROPE

Evolutionary psychologist Robin Dunbar, who specializes in studying primate brains, once determined that the amount of human individuals in a functional social group cannot exceed 150. This limit, he argued, is a direct function of relative neocortex size. In other words, we don't have the physical capacity to maintain a meaningful connection with a larger number of people because there is a shortage of drawers in our brain, where we can store all the necessary gossip.

I wonder if this rule applies to political alliances. Is there an optimal amount of countries, after which an organization becomes dysfunctional?

It's a tempting question, especially during an economic crisis that has sharpened all kinds of divisions across the European continent. Contemporary politicians speak about enlargement fatigues, ideological rifts and the failure of multiculturalism. The older electorate in Europe keeps warm memories of the time when the union was simply a community of a few prosperous countries coexisting in peace, harmony, and perpetual economic bliss.

The decision-making in Brussels was light as a breeze, Angela Merkel was still busy sorting out posters for the Free German Youth, David Cameron smoked pot at Eton, and last but not least, the participants in Eurovision were obliged to sing in their native languages.

There was a common enemy behind the Iron Curtain and the threat it constantly emanated made a lot of people, who wouldn't otherwise be natural allies, unite under a common goal.

And here's a really naughty question: Would there be a European Union if the Soviet one didn't devour the countries of Eastern Europe one by one?

It took just several years after the end of the Second World War to turn the world completely on its head. There were a lot of reinventions of old political ideas, freshly adapted to a bipolar and crudely divided continent.

Stalin, who during the war mastered Realpolitik better than Bismarck, stole the anti-Soviet idea of Georges Clemenceau and hastily started building his own *Cordon Sanitaire* of small buffer countries that were supposed to protect him from the influence of the pluralist West.

He even introduced algebra to politics, trying to persuade his capitalist ally Winston Churchill that foreign political influence in a single country can be divided in percentages among the Great Powers. According to his plan, the United Kingdom was supposed to receive a 90% influence in Greece, 25% in Bulgaria, 10% in Romania, and 50% in Yugoslavia and Hungary. The Soviet Union was supposed to cash in the rest, as if those countries were ingredients in a cooking recipe.

| Euphoric | Melancholic | Depressed |

| Classical | Modern |

| Revolutionary | Traditional |

| Sunny | Cloudy |

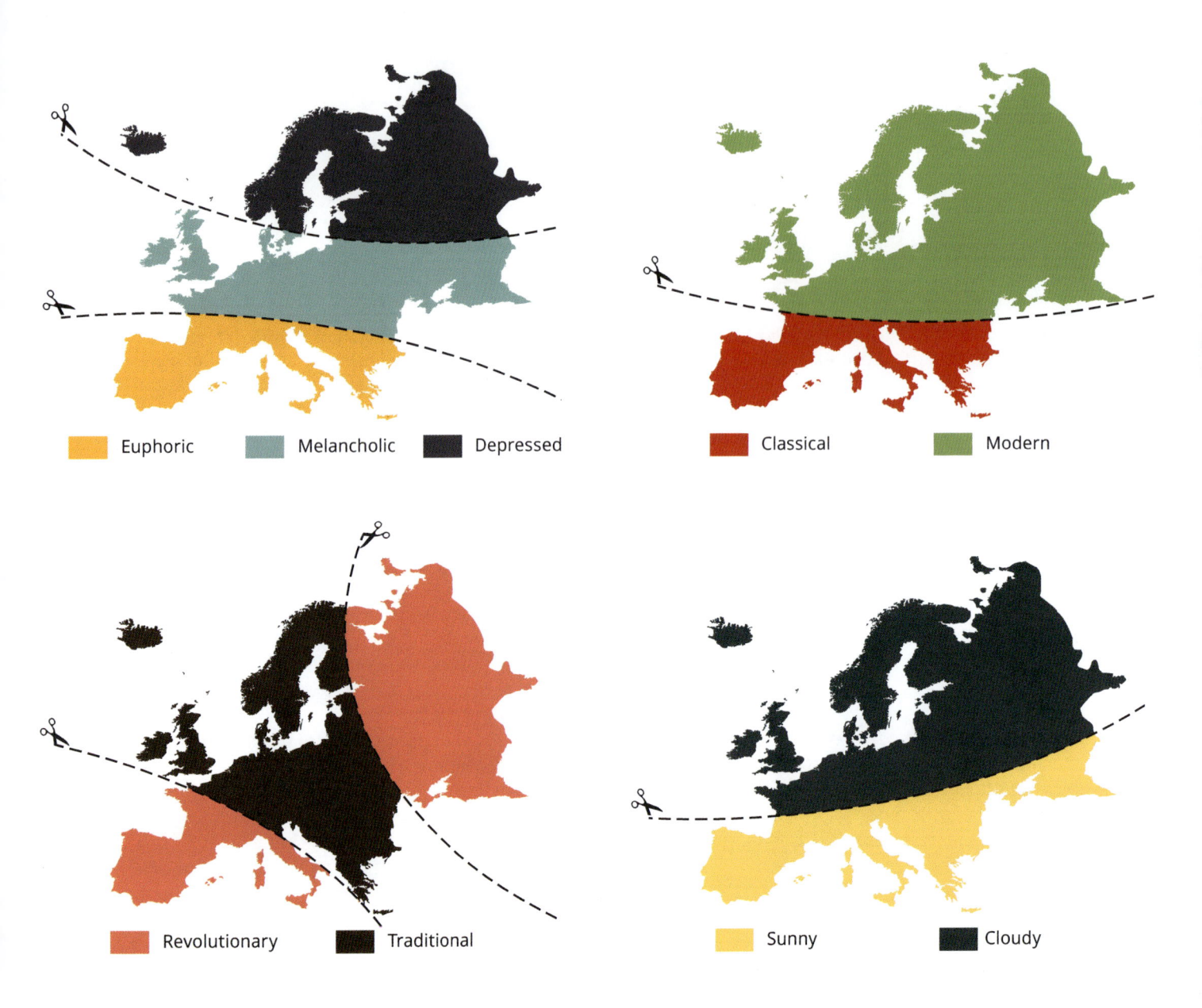

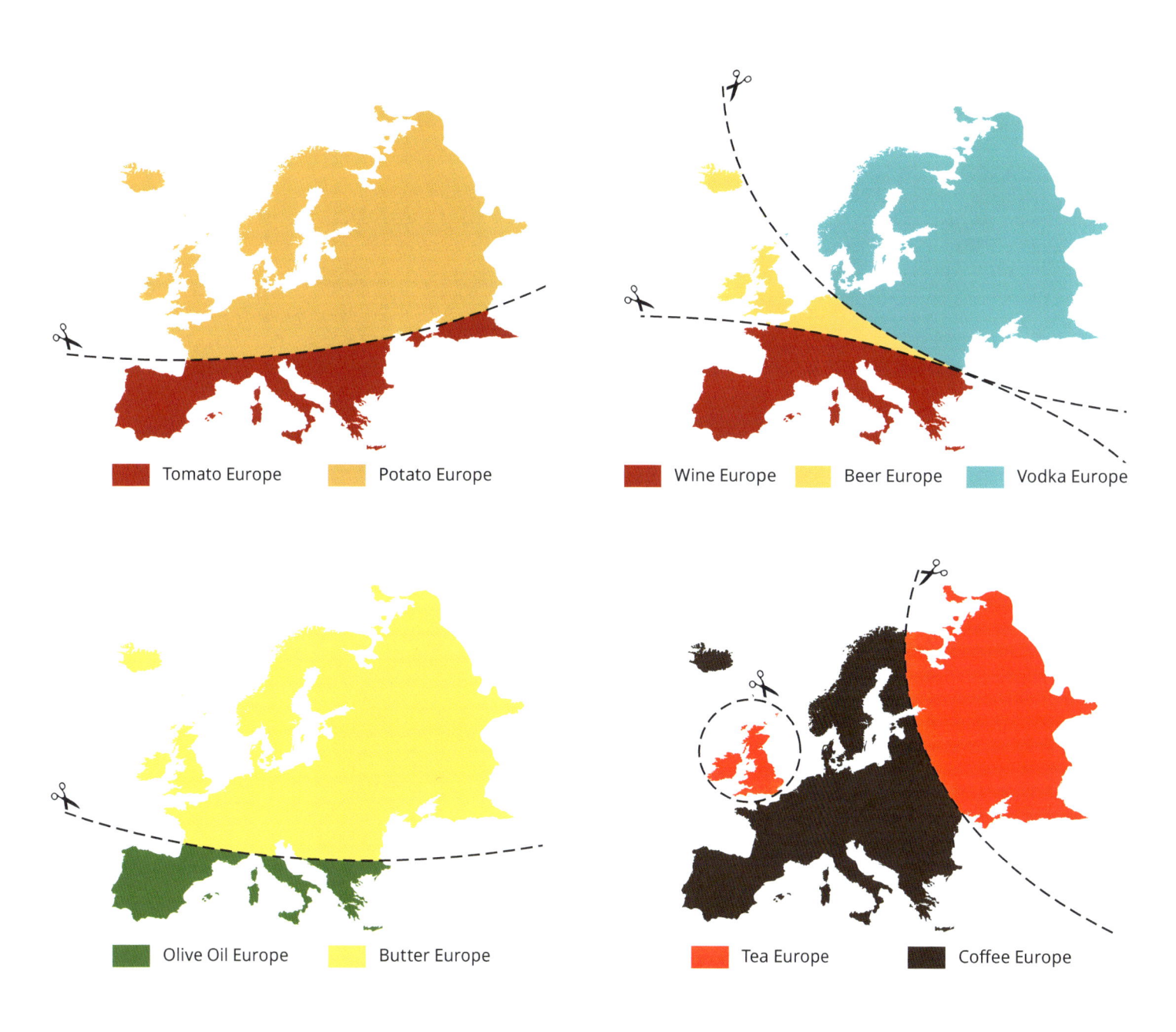

Tomato Europe / Potato Europe	Wine Europe / Beer Europe / Vodka Europe
Olive Oil Europe / Butter Europe	Tea Europe / Coffee Europe

These ridiculous calculations were just a trick to buy more time until the (not so) secret communist agents in the Soviet-occupied territories consolidated their power. Echoing the historic Defenestration of Prague in 1618, which precipitated the Thirty Year's War, the Czechoslovak foreign minister Jan Masaryk was found dead right below the bathroom window of his office. Stalin had a sense of humor darker than a black hole.

Soon every country where the Soviet percentage was equal to or above 50% suddenly got a 100% communist government, which—to nobody's surprise—didn't feel comfortable sharing power with anyone else, rendering all algebraic assurances presented to Churchill meaningless.

As a result, Europe received one of its deepest political scars, parts of which were even visible from space at the height of the Cold War.

Lush forest started popping out in the border areas between the enemy states, shaping what is now called the *European Green Belt*. Many animals, some of which belonging to endangered species, found refuge in those oases. Had the Cold War continued indefinitely, Europe would have gained back its once legendary wild forests, at least in the heavily guarded buffer zones between the two opposing camps.

There was a time when the continent was practically impossible to traverse, and such buffer zones covered vast expanses of land called *marches*. Geography, nature, and human politics flirted with each other, claiming land back and forth every time two neighboring states started generations-long quarrels. Among the notable examples was the *Spanish March*, which separated the Franks from the Moors in Iberia. Another one was the territory of modern Denmark, which even kept its original name, meaning *March of the Danes*.

While a squirrel probably had no problems traveling from Spain to Greece just jumping from branch to branch, for humans moving on dry land was much more challenging. This is why most ancient civilizations in Europe spread along the shores of rivers and seas.

The Ancient Romans were the first ones who started building permanent roads in order to keep their provinces connected. Some of those roads remain to this day. The first real cross-continental division of Europe started with the ascent of the Roman Empire.

The Romans actually managed to break Europe twice. It began with the divide between the North and the South, or as the Romans understood it, between the wild barbarians and their own superior civilization. The stark cultural disparities between those two worlds started a chain of problems for future European politicians. One of the most notable was between Hitler and his superstitious servant, Himmler, who was busy digging out prehistoric Germanic villages:

"Why do we call the whole world's attention to the fact that we have no past? It isn't enough that the Romans were erecting great buildings when our forefathers were still living in mud huts; now Himmler is starting to dig up these villages of mud huts and enthusing over every potsherd and stone axe he finds. All we prove by that is that we were still throwing stone hatchets and crouching around open fires when Greece and Rome had already reached the highest stage of culture. We really should do our best to keep quiet about this past."

Had I been a Nazi, I would have been pissed off as well. Even the most powerful rulers can't rewrite history to completely suit their own agenda. As it turns out, a pile of Roman rubble can be mightier than a V2 rocket.

The second time the Romans broke Europe was when they divided their own empire in a Western and an Easter part. What was a purely bureaucratic decision soon spilled over into a cultural and religious rivalry that would continue even to this day in various forms, some of which costing the lives of far too many people.

I am, of course, oversimplifying for the sake of humor. But I remember a serious conversation I had with an Italian friend when he took me to see Via Appia on the outskirts of Rome. After we discussed at length how this marvel of human engineering managed to survive for such a long time, he smiled and said, "This road is still intact because it was too important. It went straight to Brindisi and from there, it led to Greece. Back then almost every sophisticated thing came from Greece while people here were fascinated by gladiator fights and military engineering. In a way, the Romans were the Americans of the Antiquity."

He was also oversimplifying for the sake of humor, but his joke felt strangely apt, especially because our conversation happened at the time when George W Bush was still actively "democratizing" Iraq, while struggling to pronounce the word "nuclear" correctly.

However, even a poorly educated person like Bush knows that democracy started in Greece... presumably with the help of Jesus Christ, his apostles, and—allegedly—300 brave Spartan metrosexual men who sacrificed their lives fighting against Mahmoud Ahmadinejad.

There's an inconvenient truth about ancient democracy. First, it wasn't all of Greece that practiced it, regardless of what Hollywood movies have taught you. The cradle of democracy was Athens, one of the many city states. Second, according to the Athenians, only free males were worthy of inclusion in the term *people*, and thus it was only them who could vote and exercise power. As usual, women were considered too dumb to know what's good for them.

Below women there was another underclass with even less rights: that of the slaves. However, it's important to note that a slave could be freed and become an Athenian citizen, while no woman could ever dream of growing a penis.

These peculiarities are enough to consider such rule an oligarchy, albeit a very inclusive one. The other emblematic Greek city state, Sparta, never even thought about flirting with democracy. It was a monarchy of suicidal fanatics with a horrible cuisine. They would have certainly crashed an airplane in a trade center in Persepolis if the technology to create one was available at the time.

To the relief of Xerxes I, the Spartans failed to build a Boeing 767 and reach the Ancient Iranian capital. It was probably because they used to throw off a cliff every child who preferred mathematics to sports.

Persepolis was finally destroyed by a Macedonian guy called Alexander the Great, a student of a philosopher named Aristotle, whose teachings were almost always wrong, but just like Kim Kardashian he managed to stay famous for some reason. Alexander purposefully burned Persepolis to the ground as an act of political vengeance.

Exterminating a cultural center more advanced that your own by brute force is always a bittersweet act. Therefore Greek historians felt the need to excuse the deed and cover up the barbarism of their supposedly civilized ruler.

According to Diodorus, Alexander was simply drunk when he commanded his troops to destroy the Iranian capital. Once he sobered up, he felt great remorse. Another historian, Cleitarchus, offers an even more credible explanation. He blames an Athenian prostitute for convincing the enlightened Alexander to commit the despicable act. After all, it's not so hard to believe that every idiotic mistake in history made by great men can be traced back to evil women with mind-controlling powers.

The rivalry between Ancient Greece and Ancient Iran is often considered a milestone of the European emancipation from Eastern influence. Although the importance of this struggle cannot be denied, it would be beneficial to try to keep the myth separated from the facts.

If Europeans put aside the political propaganda, some of their successes may lose their appeal forever, but that's a price they have to pay if they real-

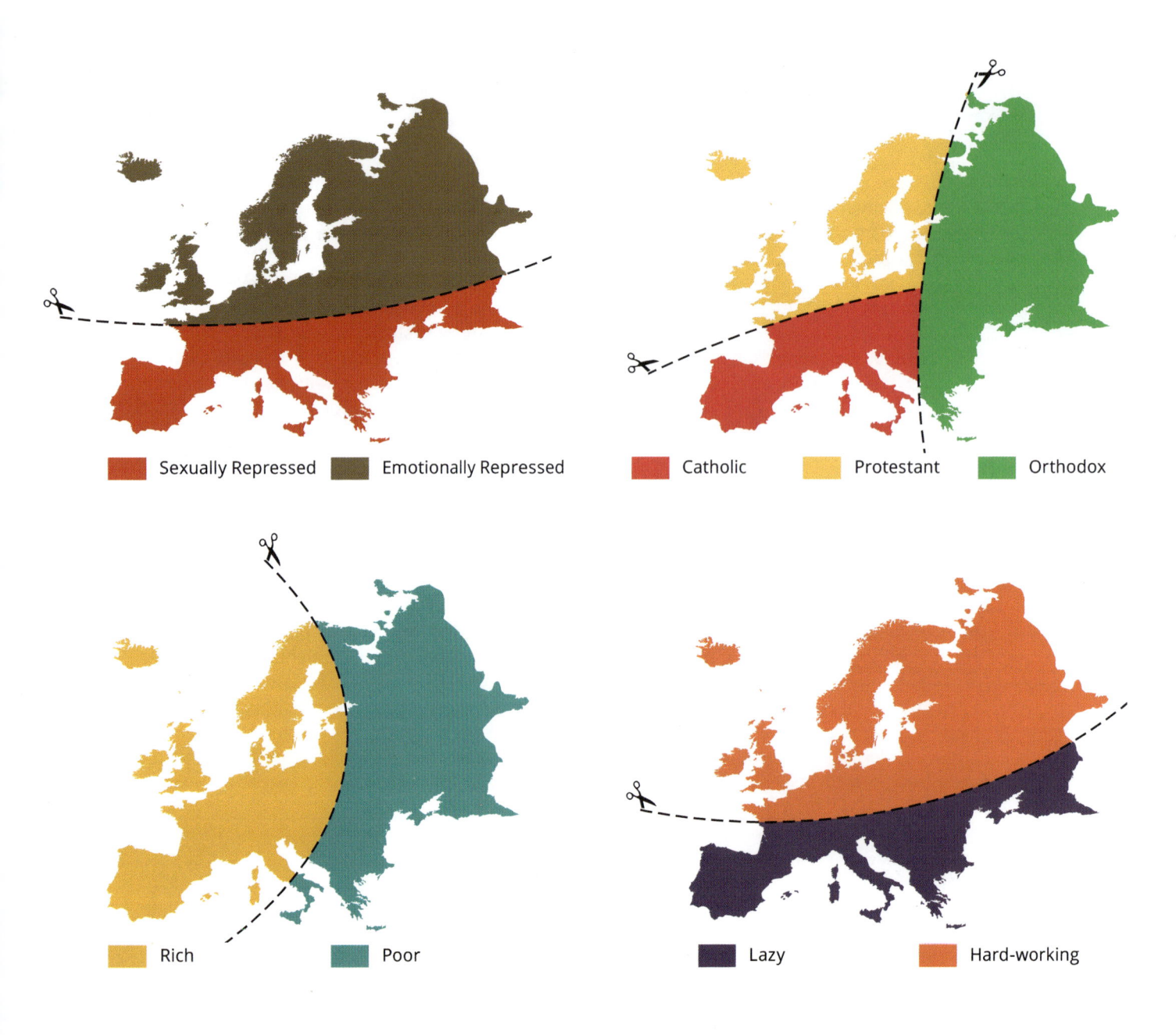

| Sexually Repressed | Emotionally Repressed |

| Catholic | Protestant | Orthodox |

| Rich | Poor |

| Lazy | Hard-working |

| Good Cuisine | Bad Cuisine |

| Deafening | Loud | Quiet |

| Fag Hags | Homophobic |

| Old Europe | New Europe |

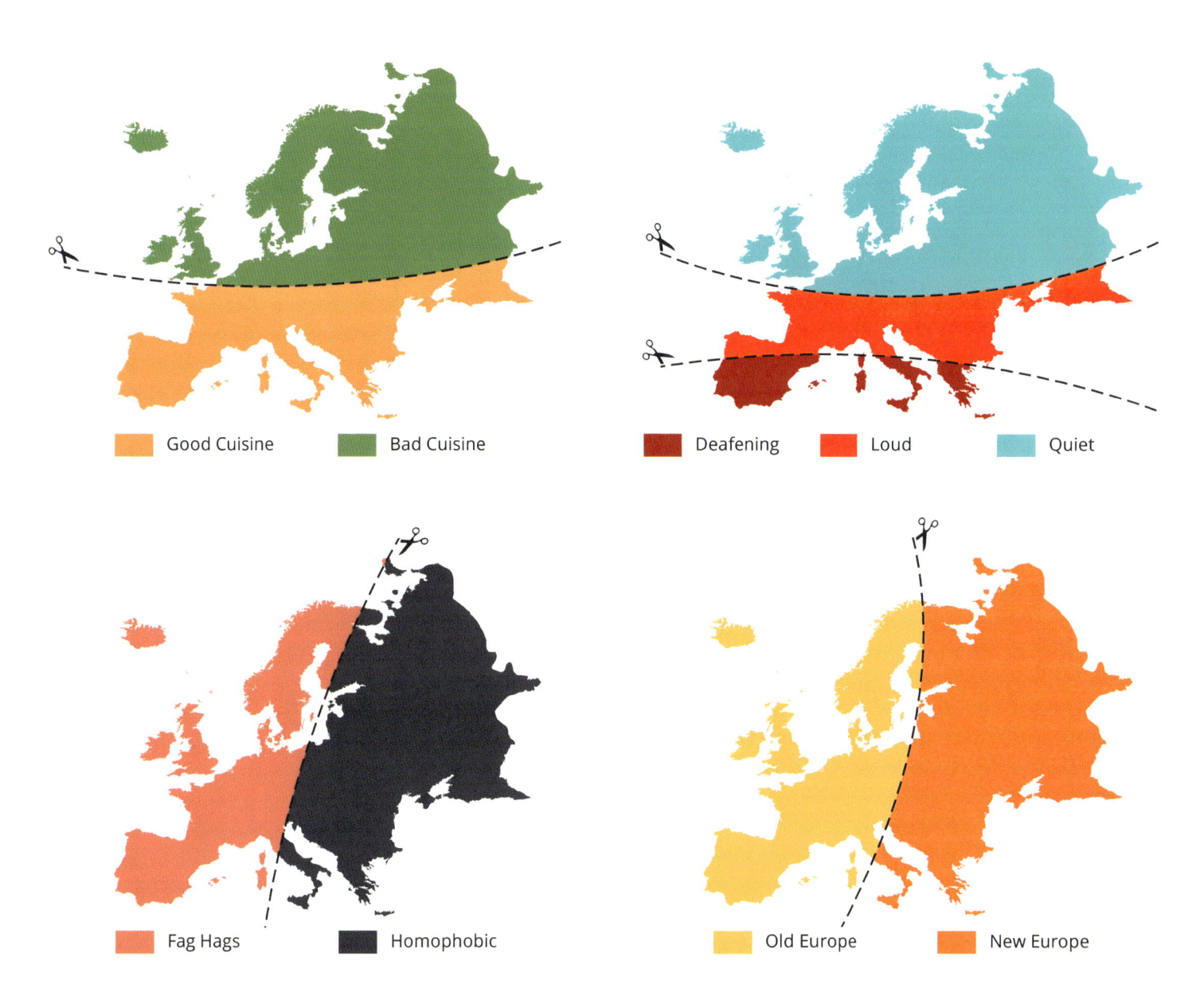

ly want to emancipate themselves. A truly civilized society cannot structure its identity using a common enemy as a foundation. It can't rely on the *us vs. them* mentality indefinitely because by doing so, its identity itself becomes a hostage. Once the enemy disappears, everything it has already built will crumble.

A true sense of unity transcends politics and a true golden age is a state of the human mind, not of the economy. A unified Europe will no doubt compete better with the rest of the world in, say, airplane construction, but that can't be a fundamental argument for integration because when airplanes become obsolete, the union will be proclaimed useless.

Reminiscing about the good old days, when economic troubles were easier to manage, is not doing anybody any good. Few things are more annoying than old people regurgitating their past. As the wrinkled neurons in their brains slowly die from sensory deprivation, their flawed memories turn to immaculate fables, rearranging the events of their lives in a brand new narrative.

While Western conservatives like Rajoy, Cameron, and Merkel flirt with austerity measures, those from the East like Victor Orbán turn to nationalism and experiment with economic protectionism.

The confusion on the left side of the political spectrum produces similar schisms. Socialists in the West struggle to reinvent Marx for the millionth time while their Eastern brothers console themselves with the memories of their communist past, suggesting that it wasn't as bad as people used to think.

Left, right, up, and down, there is a palpable sense of loss and missed opportunities. The majority of those politicians think that the European Golden Age is already behind us, hijacked by the demons of change. If only they could rewind the clock just a little bit and then hammer the arrows, so time could stand still forever and ever, just as God and Stalin intended!

Naturally, every generation overestimates the importance of its own age and thinks its values should be universal. Our shortsightedness is further amplified by the fact that we rarely take the time to truly evaluate the ideals we claim to believe in. If we did, a simple economic crisis wouldn't have been able to break Europe in pieces. We wouldn't have heard Greek people calling Angela Merkel fascist or German people calling all people south of the Alps lazy. Nobody turns fascist or lazy overnight. If both accusations are real, it means that the European Golden Age was a mirage that we only pretend to remember as reality.

The benefits of a political union dedicated to peace and prosperity are always harder to spot than that of a military alliance. A political leader who has avoided war has less chance to be remembered than the one who has won one. Perhaps it is because once a war is avoided, it gets harder to prove that it was an actual possibility, while the ruins of a disaster have an immediate emotional impact and don't require theorizing.

Contemporary Europe, with all its faults and past miscarriages, is a unique place. For the first time in history, it has managed to tear apart boundaries while keeping the sovereignty of the countries intact. This is no small feat but it's as far as any bureaucracy can go.

The rest of the so-called integration is in our own hands and it happens on a personal level. With all the borders gone, we all have access to every remote corner of the continent. We can drive, eat, drink, love, kiss, fuck, live and learn wherever we want and in the process take advantage of the best we have to offer to one another. Even those of us who fit in the crudest stereotypes have a chance for survival. A disorganized lazy Southerner can learn to work more efficiently and the pedantic uptight Northerner can learn to enjoy life a little bit better.

In 21st Century Europe everything is possible. Don't let anybody tell you otherwise.

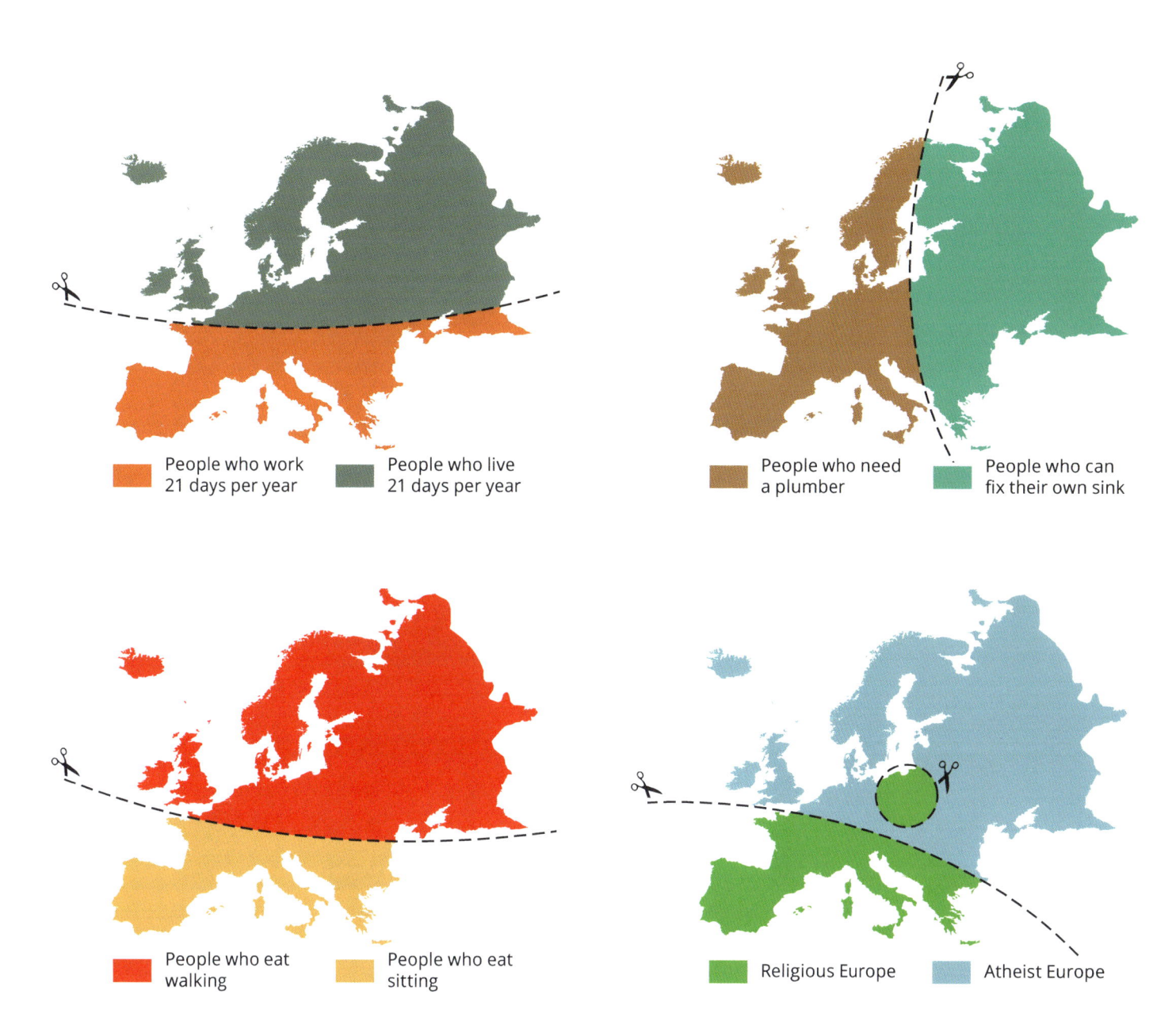

People who work 21 days per year	People who live 21 days per year

People who need a plumber	People who can fix their own sink

People who eat walking	People who eat sitting

Religious Europe	Atheist Europe

EUROPE ACCORDING TO THE NETHERLANDS 2013

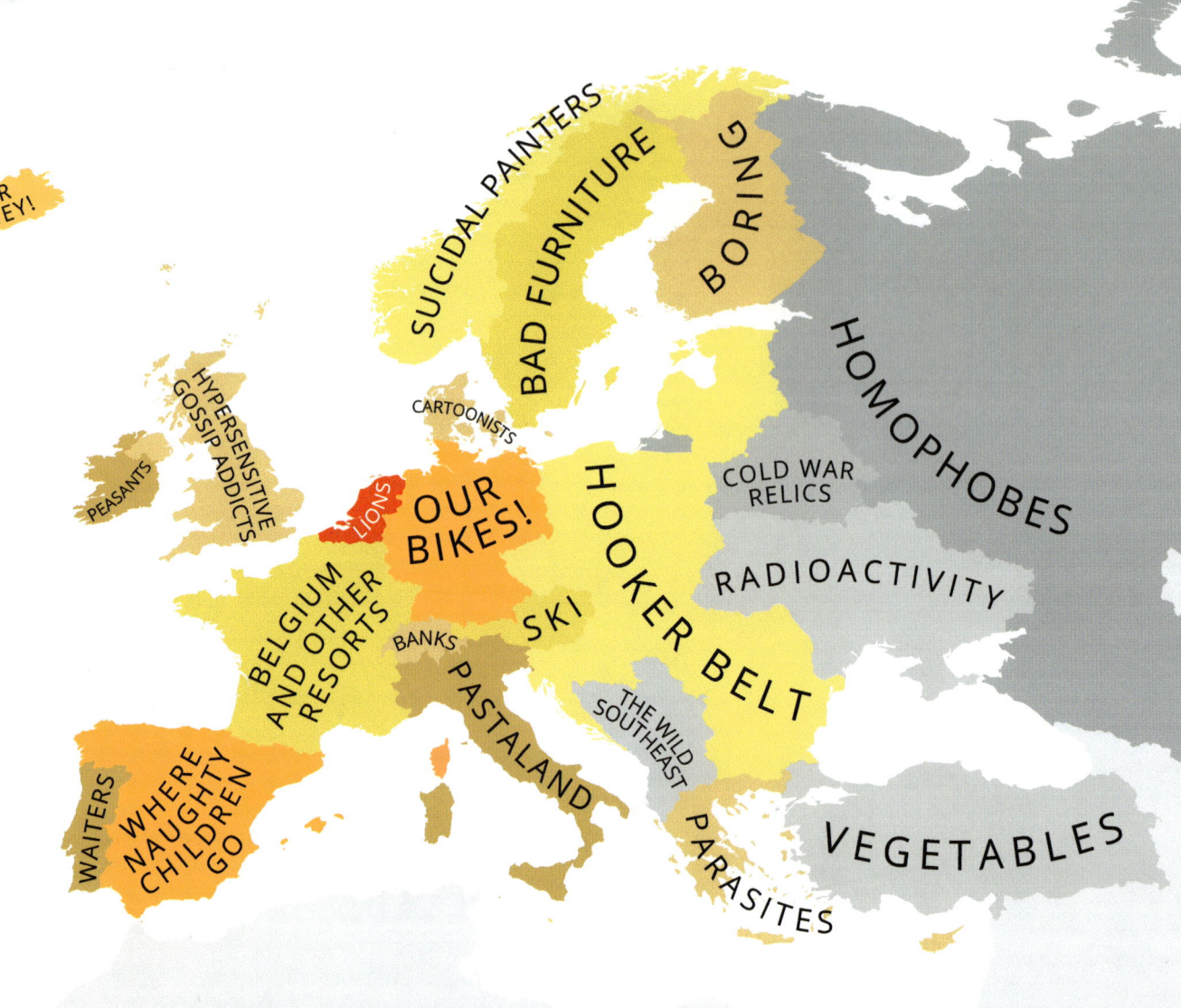

- OUR MONEY! (Iceland)
- SUICIDAL PAINTERS (Norway)
- BAD FURNITURE (Sweden)
- BORING (Finland)
- HOMOPHOBES (Russia)
- PEASANTS (Ireland)
- HYPERSENSITIVE GOSSIP ADDICTS (UK)
- CARTOONISTS (Denmark)
- LIONS (Belgium)
- OUR BIKES! (Germany)
- COLD WAR RELICS (Belarus)
- RADIOACTIVITY (Ukraine)
- BELGIUM AND OTHER RESORTS (France)
- BANKS (Switzerland)
- SKI (Austria)
- HOOKER BELT (Czech Republic/Poland/Hungary/Romania)
- PASTALAND (Italy)
- THE WILD SOUTHEAST (Balkans)
- PARASITES (Greece)
- WAITERS (Portugal)
- WHERE NAUGHTY CHILDREN GO (Spain)
- VEGETABLES (Turkey)

EUROPE ACCORDING TO SWEDEN 2013

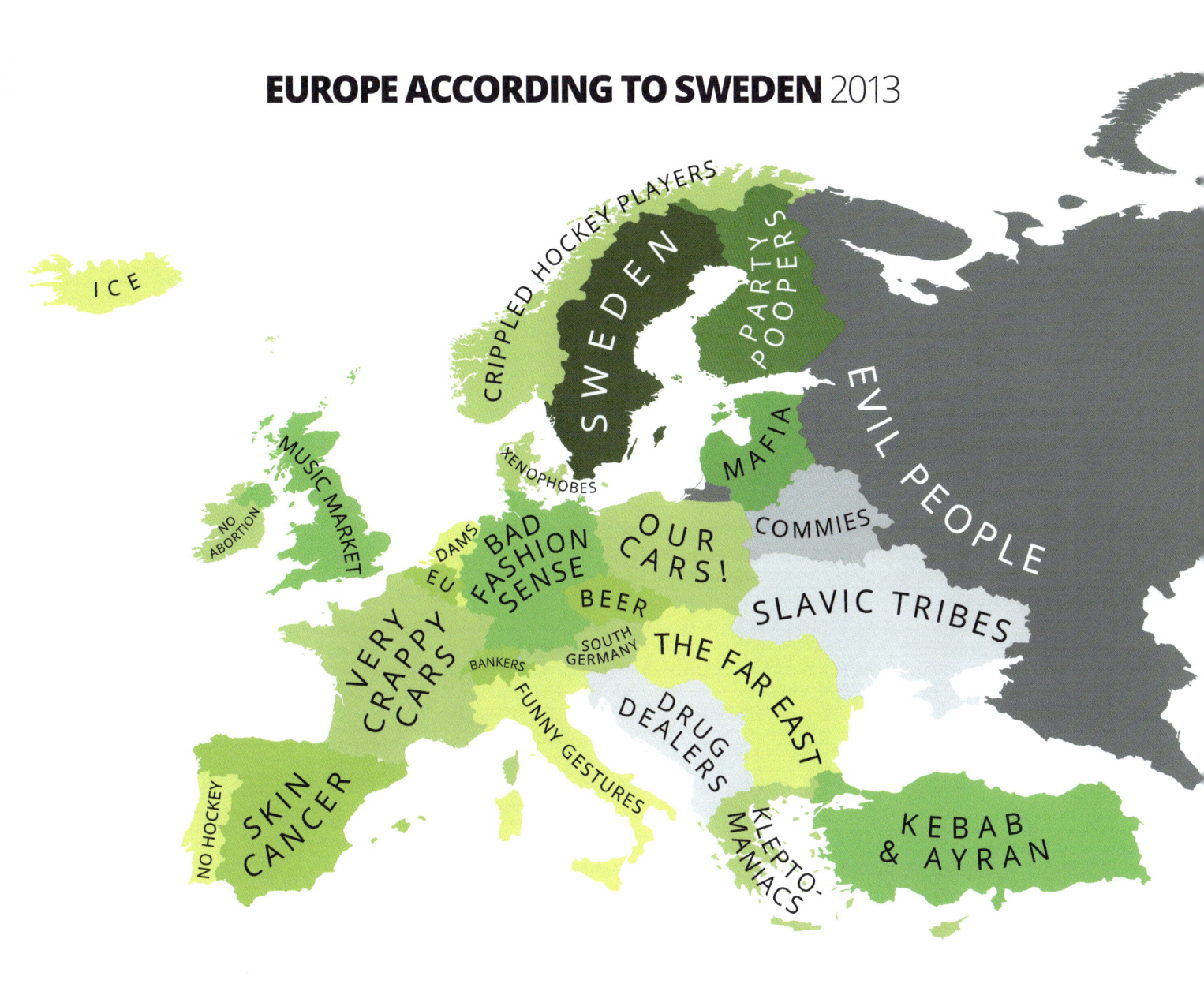

- ICE
- CRIPPLED HOCKEY PLAYERS
- SWEDEN
- PARTY POOPERS
- EVIL PEOPLE
- MUSIC MARKET
- NO ABORTION
- XENOPHOBES
- MAFIA
- DAMS
- EU
- BAD FASHION SENSE
- OUR CARS!
- COMMIES
- SLAVIC TRIBES
- VERY CRAPPY CARS
- BEER
- SOUTH GERMANY
- BANKERS
- THE FAR EAST
- FUNNY GESTURES
- DRUG DEALERS
- NO HOCKEY
- SKIN CANCER
- KLEPTO-MANIACS
- KEBAB & AYRAN

EUROPE ACCORDING TO LUXEMBOURG 2013

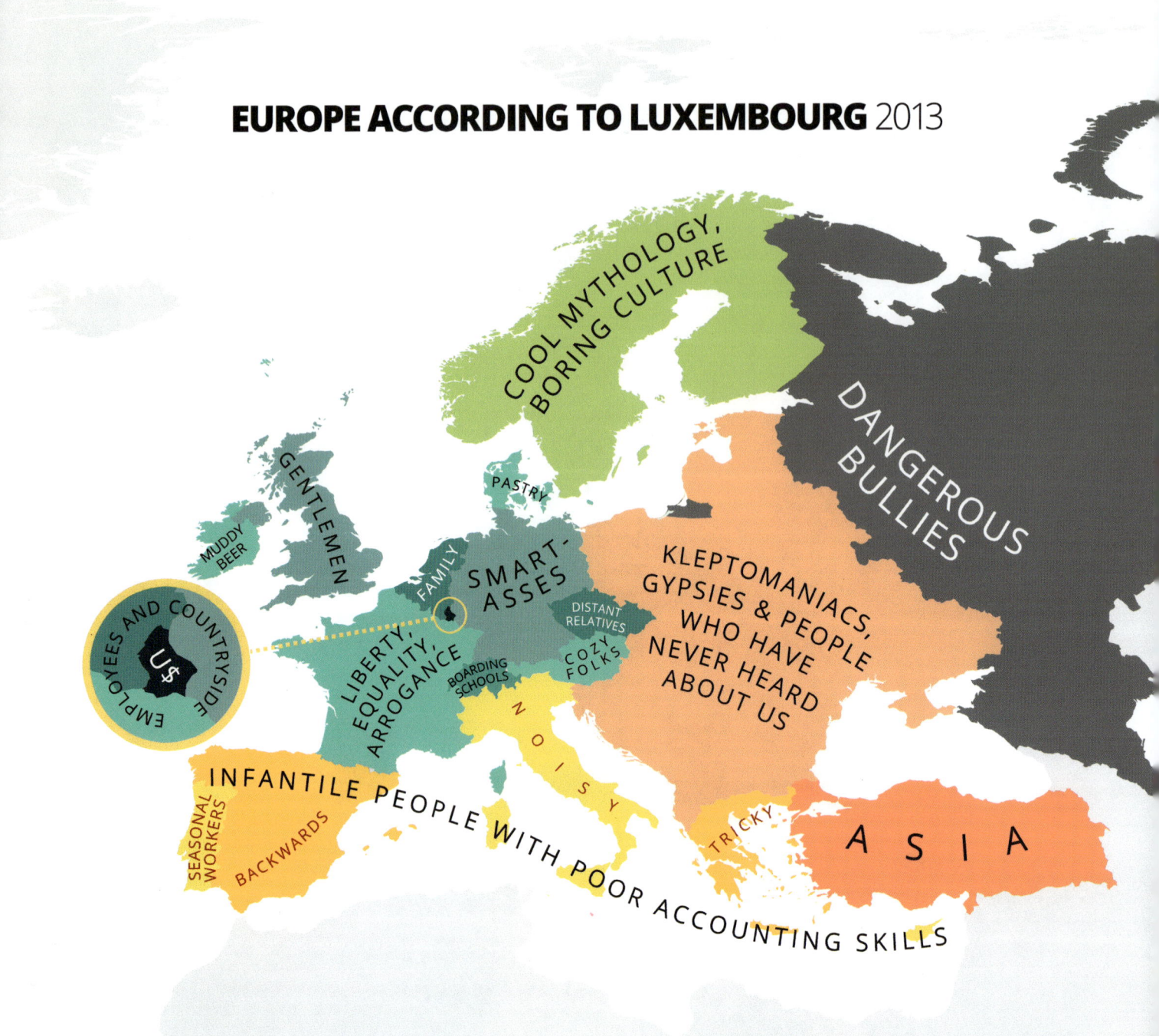

- **COOL MYTHOLOGY, BORING CULTURE**
- **DANGEROUS BULLIES**
- **GENTLEMEN**
- MUDDY BEER
- PASTRY
- FAMILY
- **SMART-ASSES**
- DISTANT RELATIVES
- **EMPLOYEES AND COUNTRYSIDE** — U$
- **LIBERTY, EQUALITY, ARROGANCE**
- BOARDING SCHOOLS
- COZY FOLKS
- **KLEPTOMANIACS, GYPSIES & PEOPLE WHO HAVE NEVER HEARD ABOUT US**
- NOISY
- SEASONAL WORKERS
- BACKWARDS
- **INFANTILE PEOPLE WITH POOR ACCOUNTING SKILLS**
- TRICKY
- **ASIA**

IBERIA ACCORDING TO ROMANIA 2013

- IGLOOS
- MISANTHROPES
- AUTISTIC BLONDES
- CIVILIZED HUNGARIANS
- IMPERIALISTS
- ACNE & BAD TEETH
- GINGER WOMEN
- FREAKS
- HOBBITS
- SOVIET UNION
- DICKS V.2
- POLITBURO
- CHUBBY WOMEN
- BEST FRIENDS
- MAFIA V.1
- GYPSY CAMPING SITE
- GERMAN SLAVS
- FORMER NEIGHBORS
- KIDNAPPED BROTHERS
- DICKS V.1
- BARBARIANS
- ROMANIA V.1
- NO IDEA
- NICE COAST
- PALS
- ROMANIA V.2
- THE BALKANS
- MAFIA V.3
- MAFIA V.2
- ROMANIA V.3
- RECLUSES
- BROKE EMPLOYERS
- CHEAP HOLIDAYS

EUROPE ACCORDING TO NORWAY 2013

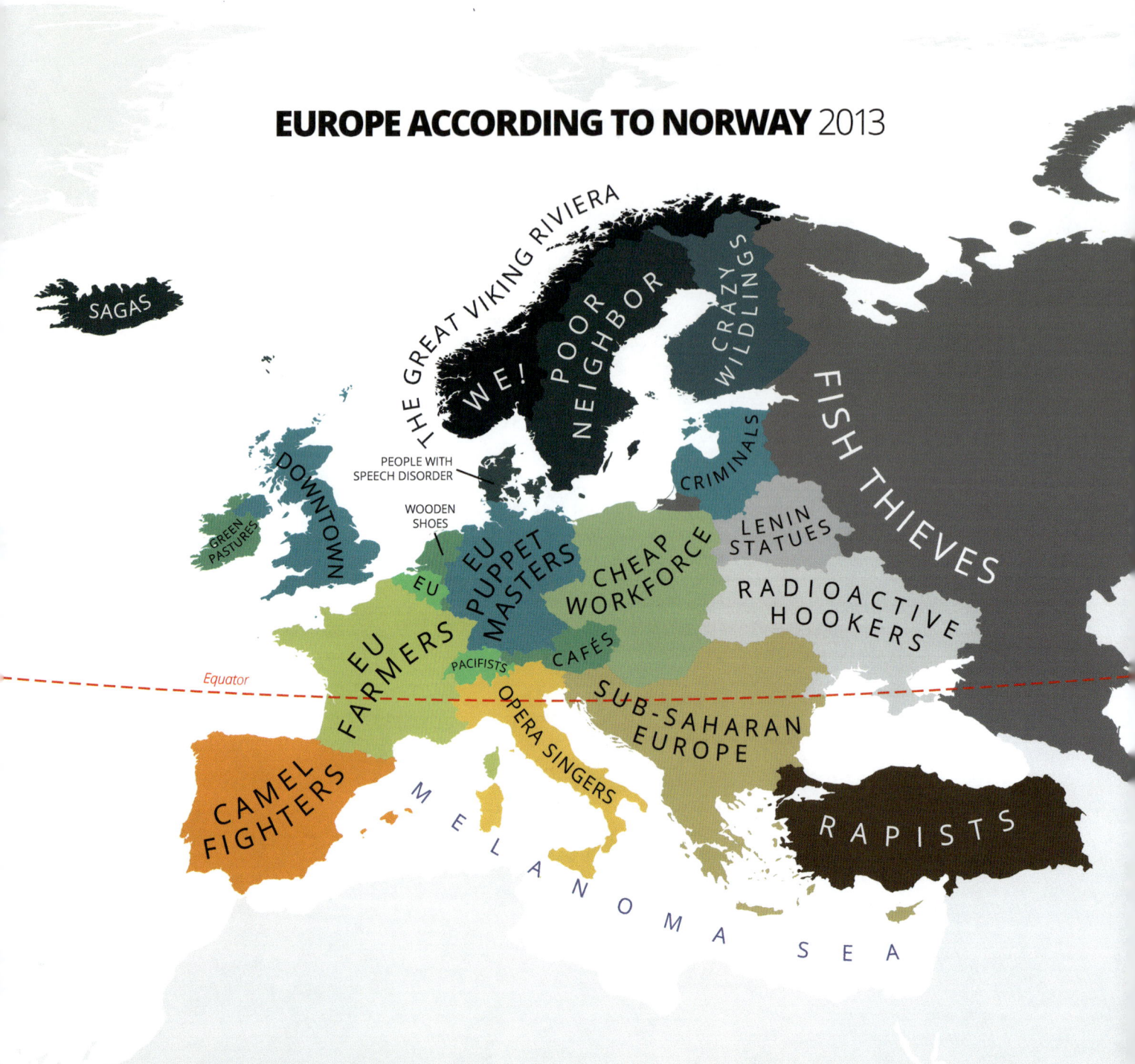

EUROPE ACCORDING TO SERBIA 2013

- IGLOOS
- JOYLESS PEOPLE
- SCANDINAVIAN RELATIVES
- ALCOHOLICS
- MOTHER RUSSIA
- IRISH KOSOVO
- DRUNKEN LEPRECHAUNS
- POSH AMERICANS
- HOMOS
- RUSSOPHOBES
- ASSHOLES
- NATO
- CAR FACTORY
- SLAVIC PEOPLE WITH THE WRONG ALPHABET
- SLOBODAN VERSION 2.0
- LITTLE RUSSIA
- SIESTA NYMPHOS
- RACISTS
- FOSSILIZED EMPIRE
- TRAITORS
- PAPRIKA
- SWEETHEARTS
- LITTLE ROMANIA
- MAFIA
- OUR EVIL TWIN
- WESTERN SERBIA
- SERBIA
- POP FOLK THIEVES
- FOOTBALL
- SERBIAN COAST
- KIDNEY MARKET
- FAMILY
- SIRTAKI
- NON-SUICIDAL MUSLIMS

ASIA ACCORDING TO HUNGARY 2013

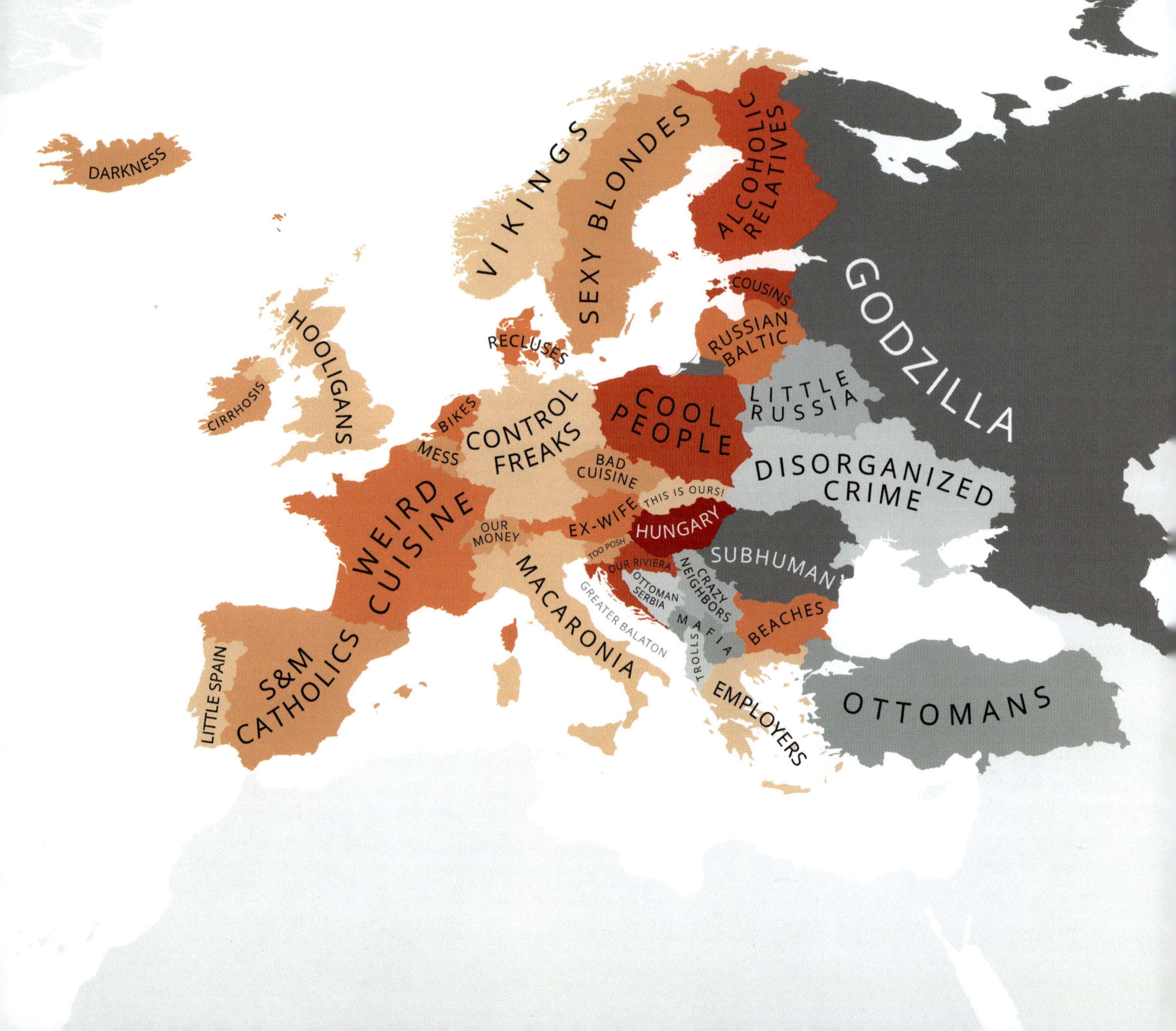

EUROPE ACCORDING TO THE BRITISH TORIES 2013

CRAWLING OUT OF PUBERTY

"The human mind is a story processor, not a logic processor," claims Jonathan Haidt in his book *The Righteous Mind: Why Good People Are Divided by Politics and Religion*. It's a secret every skilled politician knows all too well.

Raw data is the Holy Grail of science but our brains rarely enjoy it. Like uncooked food, it requires a lot of chewing before its nutrients can be absorbed by the body.

We have always relied on stories to pile up and transmit important information. One of the bestselling books of all time, the *Odyssey*, wasn't created on a typewriter. It was a masterpiece of oral tradition and was meant to be heard, not read by the public.

Because we are spoiled by the abundance of written stories today, it's very hard to imagine that somebody could remember such a gigantic poem by heart in all its hexameter glory. Yet the ability to recognize patterns, and embed information in them using a common context as an emulsifier, is a natural skill, without which human intelligence wouldn't exist, at least in the form in which we know it.

This fundamental reliance on storytelling in every human civilization, modern or ancient, doesn't come without a price. Very often the emulsifier, or the context that binds the information we want to transmit, overpowers the ideas contained within and turns into a parasite. In such cases, instead of a source of revelation, a story becomes dogma. It gets frozen in time, hollowed out by the literal interpretation of its paralyzed metaphors, which just like archaic words in a language, damage its meaning more than they facilitate it.

When such parasites start to feast on a vital mythology and the legends contained within it, the result always crystallizes in some form of institutionalized religion.

The transmission of the ideas in such religious context always requires the guidance and the approval of a specific authority, a priesthood, which role is to prevent the mummified poetry from being accidentally revitalized by some form of heresy and thus spiral out of control.

Every myth left in the hands of a bureaucrat can turn into a tool for mass manipulation. Most organized religions strive to keep the human mind in a perpetual spiritual adolescence. They actively discourage curiosity, exploration, and personal opin-

TECTONIC ACTIVITY ACCORDING TO YOUNG EARTH CREATIONISTS

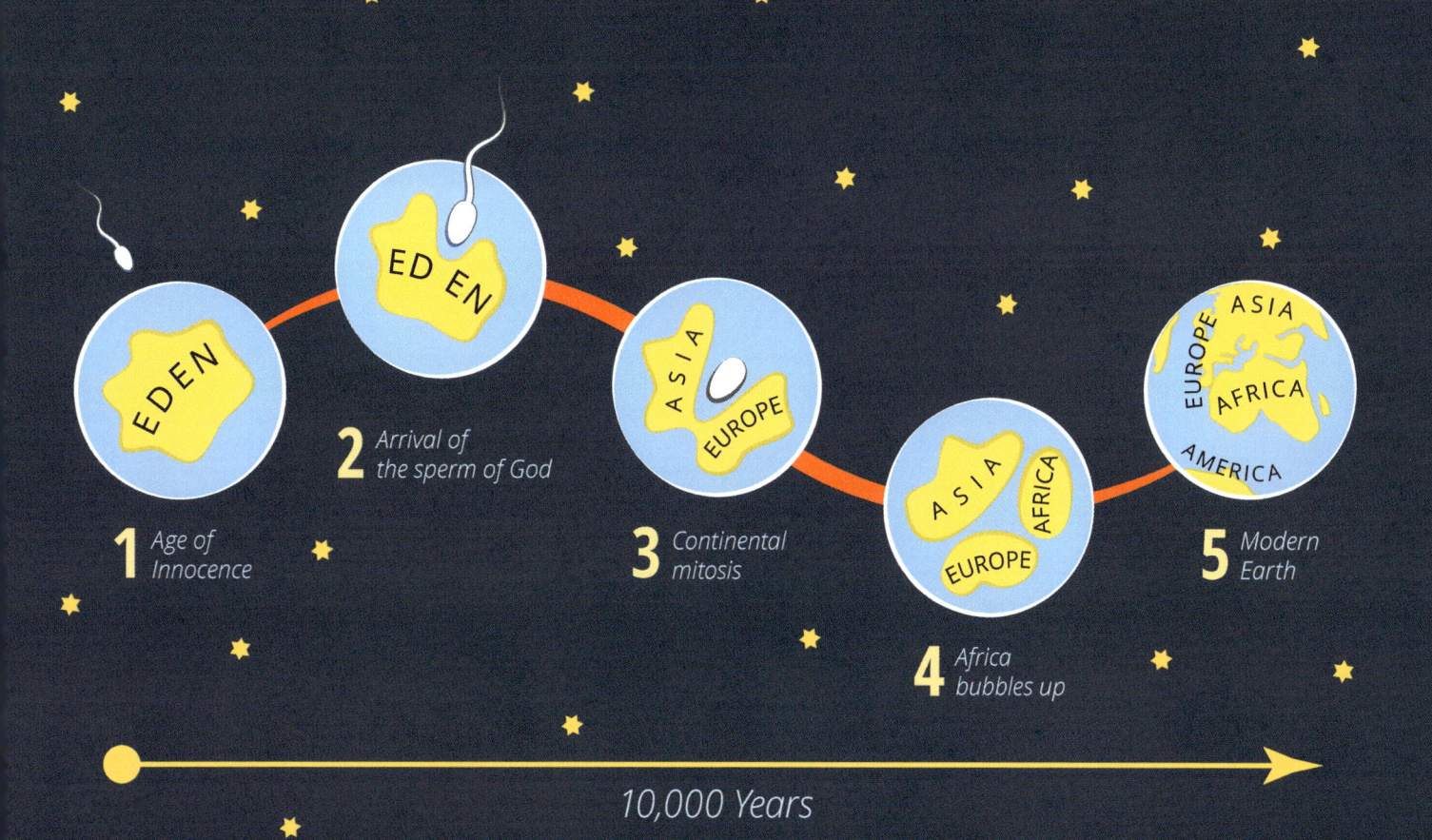

1 Age of Innocence

2 Arrival of the sperm of God

3 Continental mitosis

4 Africa bubbles up

5 Modern Earth

10,000 Years

ion, replacing them with a system of rewards and punishments designed to trigger infantile obedience and—in Christianity's case—an abundance of personal guilt, which can mutate into a plethora of mental disorders that science has yet to classify successfully.

People, who have been systematically brainwashed by organized religion and its political offshoots, often have the tendency to perceive myths in a crude, literal way. The spiritual aspect of a story, which is the thing they claim to treasure the most, is completely inaccessible to them because their minds have been robbed of the ability to understand figurative speech, the essential building block of any awe-inspiring story.

That's how Western art ended up with an abundance of frescoes featuring angels, clearly the most ridiculous creatures ever imagined by a human mind. It's what happens when people assume that Heaven is an actual place floating up in the clouds, to which you are meant to arrive in perfect physical shape. Because there were no airplanes when Christianity took hold in Europe and the Middle East, the only logical thing to do was to attach a pair of wings to the not so aerodynamic human body. All sinners proceed to gate number one, please!

Of course, the Christian angels are often overshadowed by a trademarked Muslim invention—the Heavenly virgin. She comes second only because she didn't originate in mainstream Islam but in some of its fundamentalist sects. They have a much smaller number of followers, probably because of their habit to blow themselves up with gift baskets and the occasional hijacked airplane.

The number of virgins promised to each suicide terrorist is always limited. I find that perplexing. If you're going to spend an eternity in Heaven, would an added bonus of 100 virgins make you sacrifice your life? That's only 100 nights of awesome sex. Then what?

And here's where Christianity would come quite useful, if only Muslim fundamentalists were open to a little bit of doctrinal exchange. Christianity has what every suicide bomber is dreaming of: the know-how of spontaneous hymen restoration.

We're not simply talking about fixing some post-coital wear-and-tear. The Christian god can restore a hymen that has let a baby through. Now that's a flight of the imagination worth celebrating every year as a historical fact!

Even in secular societies, driven exclusively by the values of reason, we end up pampering preachers of nonsense with the assumption that stupidity is sacred, if it carries the designation of an established religion. We carefully strive to be politically correct, lest we hurt their fragile beliefs and lead their children astray to the perils of Harry Potter worship or the Pokemon, those evil Japanese demons who, according to some American Christian fundamentalists, force children to live in a "make-believe world where they can't distinguish between fantasy and reality."

While all brainwashed religious freaks are characterized by their superhuman ability to take any type of fiction literary, they selectively refuse to believe in any kind of nonsense that doesn't come from their own scriptures.

It's not a surprise that this amazing human susceptibility to delusion has been used for political purposes both by the church and by the politicians. One of the finest examples of fear mongering comes from 1566, when a 15-year-old French woman was publicly exorcised in Laon in front of a mass audience.

Nicole Aubrey was possessed by various demons that checked in and out of her body as if it was a highway motel. Most of them were chased out by an army of experienced Catholic priests, but there was one who was particularly stubborn and refused to go away, unless it was confronted by the Bishop of Laon himself.

By the laws of Catholic serendipity, this demon was the only one with a name. To the great surprise of everybody, he introduced himself as "Beelzebub, the Prince of the Huguenots." Perhaps here is the place to clarify that the whole reality show happened during the aptly named *French Wars of Religion*. They coincidentally put Catholics and Protestants in two opposing camps, which hated each other's guts more than they loved Jesus Christ.

Nicole "Beelzebub" Audrey took her part as seriously as any *American Idol* contestant. She delivered a devastating speech, revealing the evil plans of the heretic Huguenots, who planned to do more bad things to Jesus Christ than—you guessed it—the Jews!

The word *Jew* works like a magic spell in the Christian world. The tension between Judaism and Christianity is like a family feud that turned into a blood bath because of a trivial inheritance dispute. I wonder if there is another religion that escaped the control of its own creators, only to become their karmic nightmare for more than two millennia.

Antisemitism has deep roots in the Christian psyche ,and even though the Catholic Church has taken deliberate measures to exorcise this demon in the last few centuries, its malignancy was so contagious that it broke off from the spiritual teachings and emerged as a political philosophy, reaching its climax in the monumental gibberish of Adolf Hitler and his disciples. All this happened simply because a couple of Jews in the beginning of the modern era refused to believe a guy who claimed he could perform miracles. Stupid people!

Historical irony on such a scale always comes with a grotesque price, and although events like the Holocaust may seem a distant memory that cannot be repeated today, horrible political acts fueled by decomposing religious doctrines are unfortunately still part of our daily lives.

On July 22, 2011 a grown man crashed a summer camp party, armed with a semi-automatic Ruger Mini-14 carbine and a Glock 34 pistol, and cold-bloodedly killed 69 defenseless children. This happened on a picturesque island in Norway, a peaceful and prosperous Western democracy.

His name was Anders Behring Breivik, and he wasn't a psychopath. He had a political message that was too difficult to get across, so he decided to draw people's attention to it by committing a terrorist act.

Examinations after his arrest concluded that he suffered from *narcissistic personality disorder*, a condition with a fancy name introduced by psychoanalyst Heinz Kohut. In everyday language it is usually known as megalomania, although philosopher Bertrand Russell points out a significant nuance:

"The megalomaniac differs from the narcissist by the fact that he wishes to be powerful rather than charming, and seeks to be feared rather than loved. To this type belong many lunatics and most of the great men of history."

Nuances aside, it doesn't require a university degree to understand this condition because it refers to a type of behavior that is known to every parent on this planet—the childish sense of self-entitlement and the assumption that the Universe revolves around your own ego, your own laws, and even your own personal imagination.

Breivik avoided being branded a terrorist because he was a white Christian. According to most of our prejudiced media and populist politicians, he cannot fit in the stereotype of the fundamentalist that is so carefully implanted in our heads.

In reality, there's little difference between him and an Al-Qaeda member, except probably the fact that being a Westerner, he appears to be a bit too self-absorbed to consider sacrificing his own life. Instead of blowing himself up, he gladly surrendered to the police, probably with the hope that one day some future reformed Pope will proclaim him a martyr for Christianity.

In loving memory of the innocent Norwegian children, let's make sure his dream remains a work of fiction.

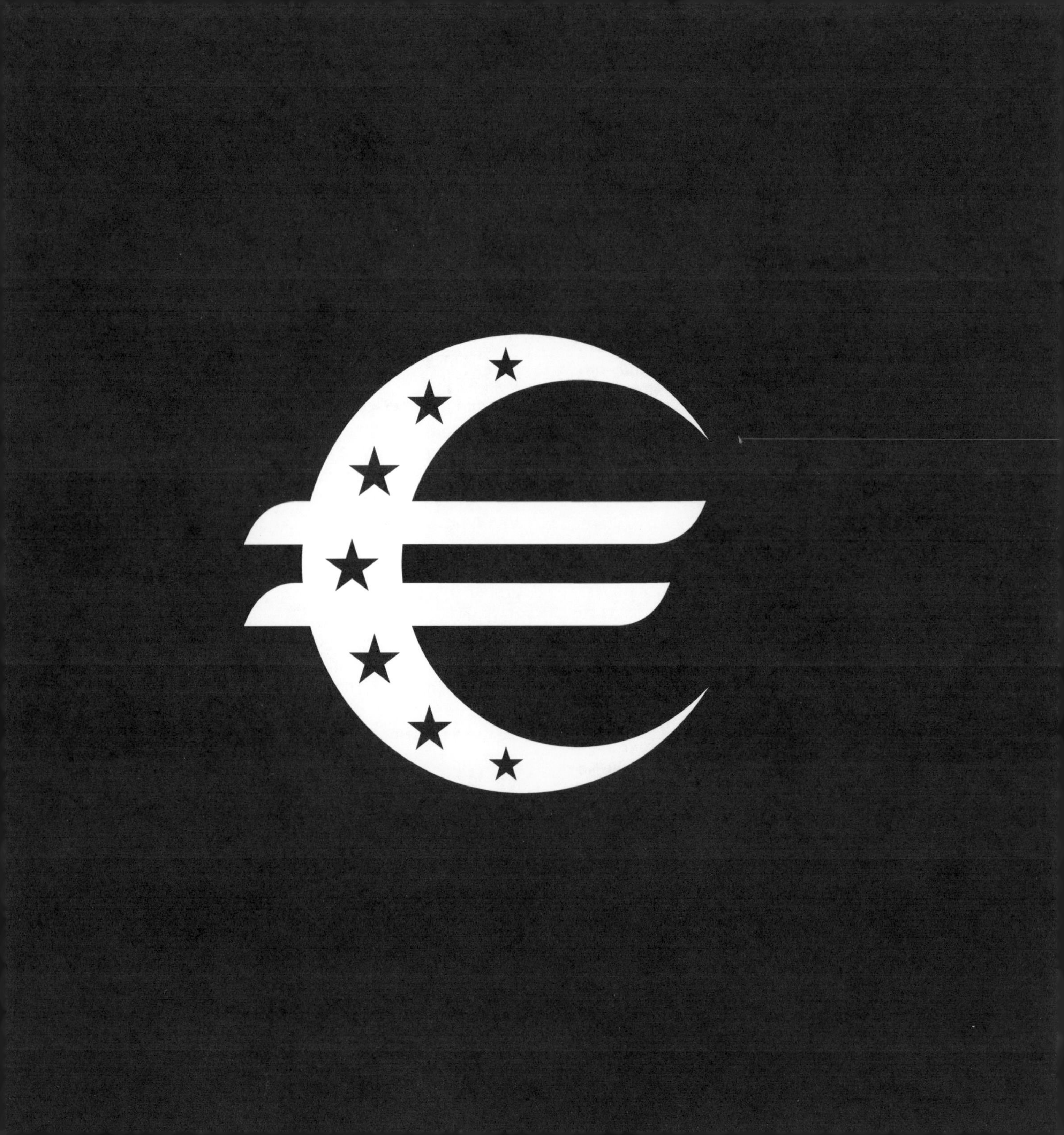

WELCOME TO EURABIA

Chemtrails spotted the sky over the bronze statue of Nigel Farage commemorating his *We Shall Fight on the Pebble Stone Beaches* speech delivered to the House of Commons several years earlier, right before a hijacked zeppelin crashed into the British Parliament and killed a flock of pigeons nesting inside.

The remains of the disaster were turned into an open-air museum by Boris Johnson's grandson, the newly elected UK prime minister. Faced with the difficult task to revitalize the wartime economy, he felt that Britain, one of the few remaining Christian nations in Europe, deserved a morale boost. Apart from the public museum with the carefully arranged pigeon skeletons on display, he completed the conversion of the last hair salons in London. They were turned into striptease clubs, where kidnapped Muslim women from the coast of Normandy were forcefully unveiled before cheering British patriots singing Handel's *Hallelujah*.

In Paris, the newly appointed Taliban mayor started disassembling the Eiffel Tower. The metal from the giant symbol of the French Republic would be later melted into swords for the Taliban soldiers in the planned invasion of Britain. The Louvre, frequently visited by members of the *Taliban Youth*, was turned into a *Museum of Degenerate Art*. It was the only place in the Taliban world where hysterical laughter was not only allowed but actively encouraged. Children who failed to at least giggle in front of the Mona Lisa were publicly flogged.

In neighboring Spain, a ten year disinfection program was just completed by the *Agency of Proper Eating Habits*, under the direct authority of the Moroccan king. Christians caught eating pork faced immediate expulsion. Those who sheltered domesticated swine had their homes confiscated and were taken into special labor camps to the south, where the greatest engineering project of the century, the Gibraltar Bridge, was in full swing.

The Sagrada Familia in Barcelona was deliberately destroyed when thousands of Muslims reported having nightmares after accidentally looking at the building and trying to figure out its purpose. A pregnant woman miscarried after she unintentionally spotted the cathedral when she sneezed so powerfully that her burka flew away and fell on the pavement. After she recovered and was released from the hospital, she was diligently stoned to death according to a clause in sharia law, which forbade pregnant women from sneezing in front of buildings with strange architecture.

To the east, Rome was experiencing a revival. The ruins of the old Roman forum were finally removed. The area got cleaned up and all the cats living inside it were castrated.

Italian men were getting progressively effeminate after the Saudi governor of Al-Apeninia, the official name of the country, doubled the amount of fluoride in the tap water. Reports of the first Italian machos growing breasts came from the area around Naples.

Switzerland, once the cradle of European direct democracy, was brutally annexed by Kuwait, and besides some newly built minarets nobody in the country noticed any difference.

The Great Empire of Kosovo conquered neighboring Austria, after the latter repeatedly refused to come to terms with its Nazi past and apologize for it. Vienna was declared the New Mecca, and all Muslims in Europe were obliged to pray facing the direction of St. Stephen's Cathedral, which was turned into a mosque.

Germany was the only Muslim-conquered country in Europe that didn't officially surrender. The German government in exile was based in China because when the Blitzjihad started, the chancellor and several of her ministers were on an official visit to a recently relocated Bavarian Weisswurst factory on the outskirts of Shanghai.

Berlin was partitioned among the wartime allies Saudi Arabia, Yemen, Djibouti, and Iran. The Brandenburg Gate was disassembled and transported to Baghdad. It was replaced by the Gate of Ishtar, moved out from the Pergamon Museum. The status of the city remains uncertain because the victorious allies split in two opposing camps after the occupation of Europe.

Only Britain, Poland, and Norway remained Christian in the aftermath of the Blitzjihad. The Norwegian king ascended to the Polish throne on an official ceremony in Warsaw, starting a personal union between the two nations. He promised to keep Polish traditions alive and extend the ban on gay marriage, abortion, and degenerate feminist propaganda.

Norway, famous for its ineffective military, escaped occupation because it hired Swedish refugees as war mercenaries. Oslo continued to be the most boring capital in Europe, even after the King unveiled a thirty-meter-tall statue of Anders Breivik in front of the Royal Palace. Its giant head hosted a rotating restaurant with a panoramic view of the city.

EUROPE ACCORDING TO ANDERS BREIVIK 2024

DEMOCRACY, TYRANNY, AND ART

While shooting the movie *The Third Man*, Orson Welles, who played the main character, decided to improvise with the dialog and added the following rant to the script:

"In Italy, for 30 years under the Borgias, they had warfare, terror, murder and bloodshed, but they produced Michelangelo, Leonardo da Vinci and the Renaissance. In Switzerland they had brotherly love, they had 500 years of democracy and peace—and what did that produce? The cuckoo clock."

It's an interesting thought, but it definitely doesn't do justice to the Swiss.

To begin with, the first known cuckoo clock was actually a possession of August von Sachsen, who, like many other provincial German rulers during the Renaissance, had a penchant for sophisticated eccentricities.

The most significant Swiss invention to date is a set of fonts, which are more ubiquitous than Coca Cola. This set was created by Swiss typographer Max Miedinger in 1957 and was named *Helvetica*, after the Latin name of his homeland.

Today, Helvetica is the de facto standard in modern graphic design, spurred by the rise of the *International Typographic Style*. Like most things that claim universal appeal, it is bland, neutral, faceless, inexpressive and unemotional.

This is exactly why it's so invisibly omnipresent. Helvetica is the default font on your iPhone. It's used in logotypes for countless popular brands like Lufthansa, McDonald's, Gap, Orange, Motorola, Panasonic, American Apparel, BMW, Target, J.C. Penney, Kawasaki, and Zanussi.

Even Arial, the font family that all secretaries around the world love and cherish, is a Helvetica rip off, Microsoft-style.

This ubiquitous typeface, and the design philosophy that underlines it, have a cult following which, in its attempt to purify modern design from any unnecessary detail, has reached a level of fanaticism that could make any suicide bomber blush.

If there is a dark side to concepts like democracy, as Orson Welles implied, it must be that sometimes, in a very ironical way, the cultures that thrive under it may develop striking limitations in their blind pursuit of compromise. By contrast, societies which are run by despotic and undemocratic principles may spark unparalleled freedom of thought.

LOST IN TRANSLATION

We often study foreign cultures relying on analogies. Backed up by intuition and experience, we assume that there is a universal set of ideas, and the only serious difficulty in cross-cultural studies is to find corresponding equivalents. Most of the time, this is undoubtedly true. As human beings, we share the same biology, the same psyche, and the same existential struggles.

But there is a catch to this cozy idea, a controversy lurking underneath, always ready to spoil our attempts to neatly organize our experience.

Take language. You can find a word for *mother* everywhere on Earth. But if you try to expand the idea of motherhood and focus on the specifics, things get a little bit tricky.

Coño is a popular Spanish curse word. It's used as a simple interjection on a daily basis. You may even drop it in front of people you just met or during a dinner with friends. According to my experience, the appropriateness of its use is pretty close to the English *damn* or the German *Scheiße*.

Yet *coño* is the vulgar synonym of *vulva*, the mysterious thing from which we all plop out into existence, and which some men fear to death. Curiously enough the word itself is masculine (nouns in Spanish have a strictly defined gender). The proper translation of coño in English should be *cunt*. But I doubt that I would ever allow myself to drop this word in a conversation with people I just met, no matter how informal it may be.

While in English there is a milder and far more acceptable way to refer to a vulva using the word *pussy*, other languages lack such lexical luxury. For example, in Bulgarian there is no way I can use an equivalent without sounding either grotesquely offensive or strictly medical. We Bulgarians often informally describe our genitalia simply as *those jobs*. It's not because we tend to be more polite or have serendipitously developed Victorian morals under five centuries of Ottoman rule. I'm almost sure once upon a time there was an extra commandment in the Bulgarian Bible saying, "Thou shalt not take the name of the vulva in vain." We stuck to it so firmly we seem to have completely forgotten that name.

The problem with cross-cultural analogies doesn't end in the realm of linguistics. Misunderstandings and false assumptions may arise in almost every subject.

Even professional historians are not immune to it. Donald Kagan, one of the biggest authorities on Ancient Greek history, has a problem appreciating the taste of olive oil.

"Some people just put [olive] oil on their salad. I myself can't stand it... If you crush the oil from the olives that come down from the trees that's a nasty smell that it has..." he shared in one of his lectures publicly available on Yale University's YouTube channel.

Professor Kagan has a rock solid reputation as a historian. He was discussing the ancient use of olive oil for hygienic purposes, explaining why people felt compelled to add perfume to it. I am sure he knows more things about the Ancient World than most contemporary Greeks. But a person who has studied the subject so extensively and has traveled around Greece (and probably the entire Mediterranean) should know that nasty is not a word that would come to mind to any local person in relation to olive oil. People don't choose it as their perfume du jour simply because nobody wants to smell of food when it's time for a party.

Even perceptions that most of us consider absolutely objective may be called into question. In Europe alone, climate varies from semi-arid to arctic. This creates a plethora of problems.

In Denmark, a heat wave is officially defined as a period of five consecutive days during which the temperature remains higher than 28 °C (82 °F). A little bit to the north, in neighboring Sweden, this threshold falls to 25 °C (77 °F). Because of such unbearable heat in the summer of 2013, a couple of male train drivers from Stockholm circumvented their company's ban on wearing short trousers at work, and boldly put on skirts, to which their employer had no objections. The risk of attracting awkward looks couldn't beat their desire to keep their hairy legs cool.

However, this is the same type of weather that would be considered mildly refreshing in Greece, Italy, or Spain, where office workers have to spend the scorching summer with their ties wrapped around their necks. On the other hand, it's not uncommon to hear Spanish news anchors speaking of *Siberian cold waves* when the outside temperature drops just below the freezing point.

A Russian and a Spaniard may argue all day long what is a bigger act of bravery—jogging at noon in the Andalusian summer or swimming in Lake Ladoga on Christmas. In reality, none would feel at all comfortable enduring the extremes of a climate which he finds unusual.

We are shaped by our environment not only culturally but physically, and every abrupt change requires a lot of effort for adaptation. Getting used to a foreign climate is like learning a new language. It doesn't happen overnight, and there's nothing you can do to force it.

Misunderstandings may arise even between cultures very similar to each other and few examples are more impressive than the different perceptions of time across Latin cultures.

While Einstein discovered general relativity for the Teutonic world only in the beginning of the 20th Century, people south of the Pyrenees have always known that time is not constant. After they colonized the American continent, Spaniards transmitted this knowledge to their new subjects, wiping out any deterministic ideas that might have existed before their arrival. In the ensued chaos, the spacetime ceased to obey the laws of physics altogether.

Today Mexicans have three different definitions of *now*. It's partially due to the magical ability of the Spanish language to create diminutives. The English word *now* translates as *ahora*. But here's where the similarities end. The Mexican ahora can last more than an hour (something which Germans might be tempted to describe as distant past). In most cases, if you want to convey the idea of absolute immediacy to a Mexican, you will have to go against your

EINSTEIN'S RELATIVITY FOR DUMMIES

MADRID (Spain)

LONDON (UK)

SYDNEY (Australia)

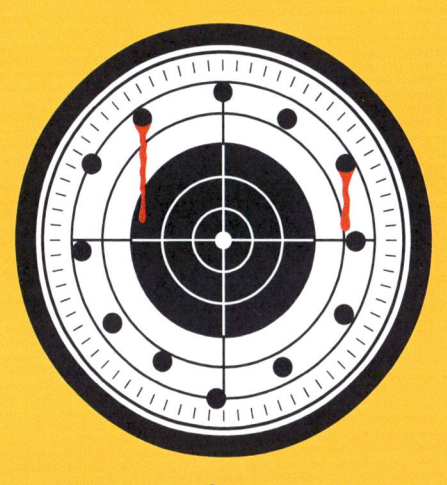

CIUDAD JUÁREZ (Mexico)

own intuition and divide *now* in even smaller units. You can achieve that by using a diminutive: *ahorita*.

Nobody knows for sure how many ahoritas there are in a single ahora. That brings up another conundrum, similar to Heisenberg's uncertainty principle in physics, which prevents us from knowing the exact position and momentum of a particle simultaneously. If you try to pinpoint the meaning of the Anglo-Saxon now using Ibero-American ideas, your ability to correctly measure time will most likely decrease. If you're stubborn enough, you may resort to a desperate solution called *ahora mismo*. Some people claim it's an even smaller unit than ahorita but I doubt it.

In the end, the only meaningful thing to do would be to loosen up and remember that what we call punctuality is an idea tailored for the machines of the industrial age, not for the human psyche.

Vocabulary is not the only aspect where temporal distortions can occur between languages. Grammar has its own wormholes that can severely affect understanding.

The grammatical tense is one of the most important characteristics of Indo-European languages. When an action is described in English, information indicating the time in which it happened is usually attached automatically. The words that describe those actions, the verbs, have different forms depending on the moment. *I am eating an apple* is different than *I ate an apple* and there's no need to add extra words like *now* or *yesterday* in order to reveal the exact timing.

English speakers are often surprised to discover that there are languages in which the grammatical tenses are used differently or simply don't exist. A fitting example is Mandarin Chinese, the most widely spoken language on the planet.

Based on such observations, economist Keith Chen suggests a hypothesis, according to which our native language profoundly influences our economic decisions. He claims that when you use English, "every time you discuss the future, grammatically you're forced to cleave that from the present and treat it as if it's something viscerally different." According to his hypothesis, this dissociation severely impacts the ability of English-speakers to foresee potential difficulties and plan for the future. To illustrate his point, he quotes statistical studies about the saving habits among people in various OECD countries. The UK and USA are at the bottom, accompanied by Greece.

Whether there is such a direct correlation between language and economic behavior remains to be proven. Simple explanations rarely manage to solve complex issues but they seduce us easily.

In Europe, the economic crisis sharpened the divide between the Catholic South and the Protestant North so prominently that it became irresistible to consider those regions fundamentally incompatible with each other. There is an enormous amount of statistics to prove such a point, yet some very important details slip through the multitude of brightly colored pie charts and infographics.

In a much publicized article in *The Guardian* titled *We Germans Don't Want a German Europe*, the financial shaman of the debt-ridden Eurozone, Wolfgang Schäuble, warned against such preconceptions: "The Germans are joyless capitalists infused with the Protestant work ethic? In fact, some economically successful German regions are traditionally Catholic. The Italians are all about dolce far niente? The industrial regions in Northern Italy would not be the only ones to bristle at that. All of northern Europe is market-driven? The Nordic welfare states, with their emphasis on social solidarity and income redistribution, certainly do not fit this caricature."

And yet here we are, scratching our heads and asking ourselves how to better understand each other. Perhaps, like everything else in life, it's the journey that matters, not the final objective.

GOING TO THE PARK IN VALENCIA, SPAIN

THE EATING DISORDER

The term *acquired taste* exists in many European languages and defines food which qualities cannot be immediately appreciated for a variety of reasons. To enjoy such meals, people often have to make a deliberate effort to get their senses accustomed to a specific smell, taste, or texture.

One can assume that, at least from a biological point of view, all tastes are acquired except that of human milk, to which babies are instinctively drawn from the moment they are born. Ironically, it is the only taste that has to be forcefully relinquished. Giving it up is an essential requirement in the process of growing up.

Milk appeared in nature specifically as food for babies. Therefore, it's not a suitable source of nutrients for adult mammals. The vast majority of the animals that feast on milk in their infancy lose the ability to digest it after they reach maturity and become independent.

Being human, we have found a way to circumvent this evolutionary obstacle by adapting our digestive systems. But interestingly enough, we shun our own milk and prefer that of domesticated animals, to which we got accustomed simply by accident.

Yes, we would rather prefer to suck the tits of a cow than those of our own females. To make things borderline grotesque and slightly pathetic, in some puritan cultures like the American one, public breastfeeding of babies is considered a scandalous taboo. Just ask Barbara Walters!

Confusing and counterintuitive as it may be, this is just the tip of an enormous culinary iceberg. The things we eat, and the tastes we get accustomed to, have more to do with our immediate environments, cultural backgrounds, and spiritual aspirations than with ordinary biological factors.

National and racial prejudices go hand in hand with culinary ones and often blend together. Ridiculing foreign cuisine is a favorite pastime of close-minded people all over the world.

But even those of us who consider themselves open-minded may occasionally fail to recognize the value of a culinary challenge. Food, just like language, has the power to directly shape our identity. Smells and tastes leave imprints in our minds. They often acquire an emotional context, and become inseparable parts of our memories.

Food preparation can be a long, complex ritual, passed from parents to children with the comforting hope of preserving a collective identity. There are countless legends of secret recipes shared only among very close relatives, preferably on a deathbed, after a priest has administered the last sacrament.

Food is also part of our religious experience. It can be argued that it is a central factor in our mytholo-

CULINARY HORROR MAP OF EUROPE 2013

gy. The most ancient religious doctrines started as attempts to imitative nature, or more precisely, that aspect of nature which had an immediate connection to people's nourishment.

The hunter-gatherer societies developed the cult of the animal spirits that dwelled in the forests where they found their food.

The agricultural societies of the Middle East and the Indus Valley started worshiping the plants, setting the rules of a game we continue to play today by burying our dead in the ground with the hope that they will be reborn.

All major religions in the world have strict rules about what should be considered food and when it should be consumed. Those rules are not based on pure reason but are a consequence of socio-economic demands. Some can be astonishingly absurd. For example, the Catholic Church classifies beavers as fish. This awkward decision was taken four centuries ago, after it became clear that the baptized Native Americans around Quebec wouldn't give up eating beaver meat during Lent simply because of their newfound love for Jesus Christ. The Church had to adapt or expose itself to the risk of another wave of Protestantism, this time coming from the New World.

Yet food can be an incredibly mundane thing. After all, it's something we put in our mouths, digest in our guts and shit in our toilets. Everything we consider special about it exists only in our heads.

The human brain is the most energy-demanding parts of our bodies. It will do everything to trick us to provide it with nutrients. Our brains will fire signals to the right neurons and pump us up with chemicals that will make us salivate. They will emotionally blackmail us with artificial concepts like *comfort food* or *delicatessen*.

Remembering this trivial fact is essential for maintaining a healthy relationship with our food. Like mythology, food serves us best when we are aware of the illusions it can inspire and the delusions it can create.

We Europeans are often proud of our national cuisines. We also tend to assume that disgusting food can be found exclusively in foreign, "exotic" cuisines.

This is a gross misconception. Europe is littered with disturbing domestic meals. There's a vast selection of fermented fish in Scandinavia, offal stews on the Balkans, deep fried pizzas in Scotland, sadistically squashed birds cooked under pressure in France, and a variety of dishes made of animal blood across the entire continent.

The top spot is reserved for Sardinia, where a special type of sheep cheese, infested with semi-transparent insect larvae, will tickle all your senses in a way you won't forget.

The opposite is also true. You can find something delicious in every European cuisine. Good Old Britain, object of constant culinary ridicule, has its *English breakfast*, which even French people dare to praise, although under the condition of anonymity.

Sadly, delicious food and satire don't mix well. Have you ever tried to ridicule a Schwarzwald cake? Go ahead and tell me how it went!

GENERATION ME

Beyoncé surprised everybody last night when she suddenly released her fifth album on iTunes. According to her PR team, it's a spontaneous act that liberates her from the marketing cycle through which record companies suffocate artistic authenticity. She's now, in her own words, connected "directly to her fans."

Of course, she's still signed to a major label, and there isn't anything revolutionary in the album production itself, but those mundane details got lost somewhere between the email servers of her publicist and the mailboxes of music critics.

Did I say critics? I tried to find a review of the album and Google presented me with a selection of high-profile media outlets: *CNN, Billboard, The Guardian*... Caught off-guard, most of the reviewers simply offered extended reports on the news. Yes, they said, she has a new album out; every song is accompanied by a music video; it's probably spectacular but it will take time until we can be absolutely certain about it.

Wait! Was that what I wanted to read? Did I just do a Google search, only to find what I already read on Twitter hours ago? Apparently not. *The Guardian's* Rebecca Nicholson had a little extra. She actually read her review in front of a camera and called the album a "brilliantly strange record," a statement as opaque as a UN Middle East peace roadmap.

But I digress. The interesting thing is that, musical tastes and marketing strategies aside, Beyoncé not only created an "immersive" video album experience. She also managed to inspire critics to spontaneously grab a camera and add a splash of vision to their writings.

The last century ended with Andy Warhol's prophecy granting everyone their 15 minutes of fame. The 21st Century turned out to be far more generous. The time restrictions Warhol put on fame are not valid anymore. They were a consequence of the broadcast mentality of the Television Age, when they day had 24 hours and was partitioned among few competing A-listers. Today everybody is a star, simultaneously and perpetually. Even critics.

Critics are not interested in being a corrective force because the whole notion of an established authority is not cool anymore. What's cool is your hairdo, your gadget, and the rasterized quotes by famous people you share on Facebook and Twitter, with an added personal "wow" at the end. The systematic effort, that vital element of getting things done, has been replaced with the declared intention. Everything is a tap and a click away.

The lack of authority created a vacuum to which we still struggle to adjust. The mind-blowing speed with which information travels leads us to believe that what we see in our newsfeeds is a stream of everything significant going on in the world. Few of us are aware that social networks, content discovery services, and even search engines like Google meticulously try to analyze our habits. By filtering out subjects that are unknown to us, they use algorithms to serve us information tailored specifically to our taste, filling the empty gaps with "useful" automatic recommendations from our contacts.

Internet activist Eli Pariser calls this phenomenon a *filter bubble*. It could potentially introduce a new kind of world view, a quantum mechanical nightmare where each of us perceives a personalized version of the Universe based on the specific information fed automatically to our brains. It may seem like science fiction but it's not hard to spot examples which are disturbingly real.

"A world constructed from the familiar is a world in which there's nothing to learn," writes Eli Pariser in his book *The Filter Bubble: How the New Personalized Web Is Changing What We Read and How We Think*. The contemporary music industry, and its focus on pleasing established tastes, is a brilliant example, with or without its hype-generating antics.

However, the detrimental effect of the authority vacuum doesn't always involve a filter bubble. It could appear as a good old misinformation tsunami.

Nelson Mandela died just days before Beyoncé's exotic marketing stunt sent ripples across the Internet. The event created a media storm in which the smallest details were blown out of proportion. Journalists all over the world milked every public statement, trying to captivate the eyes and ears of an audience with a notoriously short attention span.

A day later, attending the memorial service in South Africa, Barrack Obama had the audacity to take a selfie with David Cameron and Helle Thorning Schmidt, prime ministers of the UK and Denmark. Hordes of outraged Twitter users voiced their disapproval, copying and sharing false information, according to which the act happened during Mandela's funeral, an event that was yet to take place.

Some British tabloids paid special attention to Michelle Obama, who seemed to frown disapprovingly at the alleged disrespectful behavior of her husband, prompting a debate about the unjust stereotype of the "angry black woman."

On December 15, 2013 it snowed in the Egyptian capital Cairo for the first time in 112 years. As the news of the extraordinary event spread, pictures of the Sphinx and the Giza pyramids covered in snow were shared more than 10,000 times on Twitter. They later turned out to be fakes but the number of people who found out about it was significantly fewer.

Misinformation spreads with such ease on social networks because everything we see in our newsfeeds is taken at face value. It usually reaches us via friends and family, people who we implicitly trust or feel compelled to agree with. In such a scenario, the open-mindedness, which the Internet is supposed to inspire, can easily turn to mass delusion.

Some delusions are harmless. There is little danger of something bad happening just because you've been misled that the snow in Cairo didn't reach the pyramids, located 20 km southwest of the city.

Things can get scarier when you see your friends sharing bogus medical advice without checking the credibility of the source or consulting a professional. Made-up diseases like "inflammation of the immune system" are diagnosed by people who can barely distinguish a liver from a stomach. In another post, you can be asked to save a little baby whose successful cancer treatment is funded by likes and shares.

The dream of a more informed, elevated society can dramatically degrade into a dystopia where ignorance and narcissism reign supreme. For some, this dreadful outcome is already a reality. *Slacktivism* is a term describing our addiction to parade values with minimum effort. Want to help a demonstration in Iran? Change your profile picture! Outraged by India criminalizing gay sex? Sign a petition, and ask your friends to join in!

THE WORLD ACCORDING TO A FACEBOOK USER

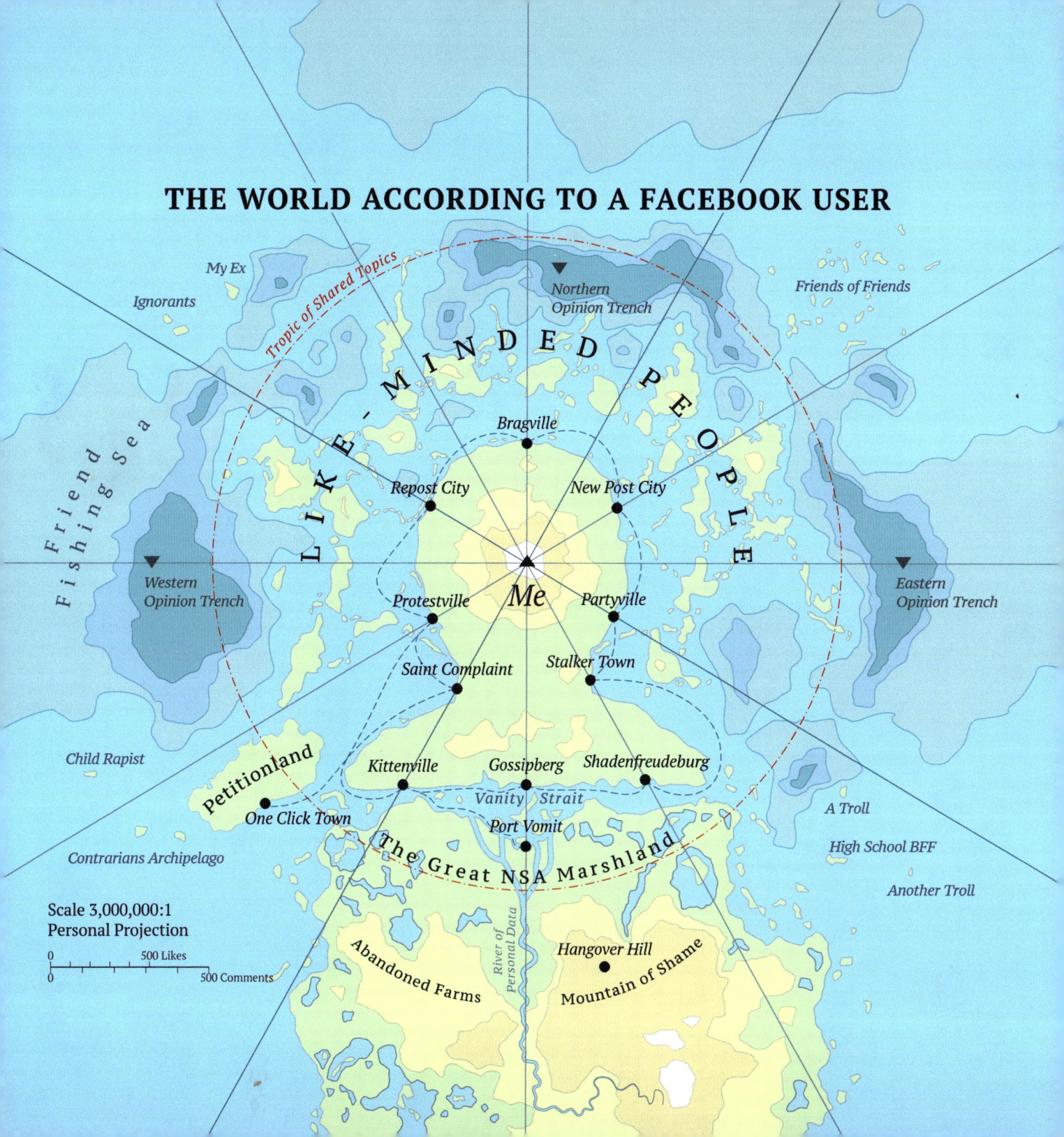

The dissonance between declarations and problem solving became especially apparent in many protest movements from the beginning of the decade like *Occupy Wall Street* in the US or the *Indignados* in crisis-hit Europe. Both movements demonstrated an amazing ability to mobilize people and organize protests. What they didn't do was offer successful alternatives to the political order they so enthusiastically condemned.

In the meantime, our obsession with fame turns every just cause worth fighting for into cheap demagogy. A telling example is a recent royal pardon, granted posthumously to UK scientist Alan Turing, who was sentenced to chemical castration in 1954 simply because he was gay. Not a word was uttered about the other 50,000 victims of the *Gross Indecency* law, many of whom were submitted to the same barbaric treatment.

As the tsunamis of misinformation spread to the most remote corners of the world, our narcissistic idealism grows like a mushroom in freshly piled manure. By condemning everything imperfect, we have become trapped in our own fallibility as human beings. We have forgotten that ideals should be perceived as guidelines, not as attainable goals that can materialize out of thin air.

All men are pigs, said a woman. All women are bitches, said a man. Thus the human race got extinct.

ABOUT THE AUTHOR

The older I get, the more I realize that biographies are a waste of time. Let's face it, when it comes to books, the only people interested in biographies of authors seem to be lazy journalists or neurotic fans. Both bore the hell out of me.

Lazy journalists will mess up an article no matter how structured is the information you provide. In a single year various publications managed to write that I am 36, 37, and 38 years old. One insisted I was 43. Even my publisher got the year wrong. I'm not complaining though. The age of an author is a boring detail nobody should pay attention to and those mistakes are the best evidence for it.

Then there are the neurotic fans who write you poems telling you what a wonderful human being you are without having even met you in real life. That's sad. It's one of the ugliest examples of our manic obsession with celebrity and fame. Have such people ever admired an idea instead of a person?

When I get overwhelmed by such dark thoughts, I find refuge in astrophysics. According to it, one day the Sun will explode and the Earth will boil away, together with the entire Library of Congress.

I know some smartass billionaire will manage to build a space capsule, fill it with his precious spermatozoids and shoot it towards Alpha Centauri right before the disaster. It may even beget another civilization, much more advanced than our own. But then again, one day the whole Universe will die. Space itself will stretch so thin that subatomic particles will spill their guts and evaporate away into the Great Nothingness.

Just imagine the relief! All the clutter we piled up for millennia – gone! My book was a bestseller? Oh great, look at it vomiting neutrinos all over the place until it dematerializes completely.

So let's keep it simple. I am Yanko. I live in the now. That's my biography.

NOTES AND THANKS

Writing books is difficult but so is publishing them and making sure they reach the right audience at the right time. There are many people involved in the process. Martin Brinkmann, my agent and editor for the German edition, is one of them. I have probably tested his patience many times during the long creative process. I already missed 3 deadlines and he hasn't complained a bit. That's good karma. I'm sure he will skip at least one reincarnation cycle because if it.

Next in line is the team at Knesebeck, my German publisher. I know perfect publishers don't exist but I can't seem to find any fault in them. They never complained about the deadlines as well. This is weird because most Germans I know are obsessed with punctuality. To give you an idea: my German teacher in school always refused to let anyone in the classroom after her. It didn't matter how much you were late, it could be just a fraction of a second.

If the people at Knesebeck are alike, they hide it very well. And I want them to know that a) I am deeply ashamed of being repeatedly late, and b) there's a virgin in heaven waiting for each and every one of them!

Another team that has contributed enormously to the success of this book series is that of Galina Dursthoff and Alpina Non-Fiction, my Russian publisher. They helped me reach an audience I have never imagined I could!

No decent book has ever been written without a muse and no decent idea has ever evolved without a friend to share it with. Emiliano Barragán-Géant played both roles perfectly. He is responsible for keeping my eyes open and my personal prejudices—in check. Many of the essays in this book were sparked by our endless conversations and discussions about food, religion, music, magic, and love.

THERE'S MORE WHERE THIS CAME FROM

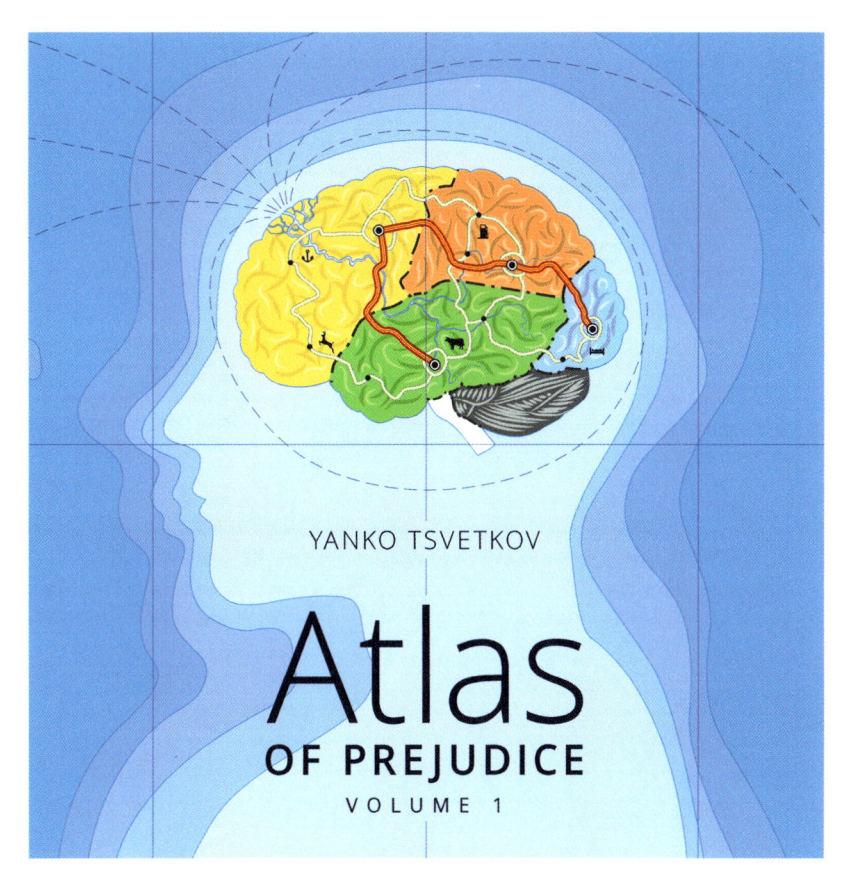

YANKO TSVETKOV

Atlas
OF PREJUDICE
VOLUME 1

The first volume of the *Atlas of Prejudice* was published in four languages and sold more than 20,000 copies worldwide in less than a year. The book is available from Amazon in the USA and its regional stores in the UK, Germany, France, Spain, Italy, Japan, India, and Canada. It can also be purchased from other online retailers like The Book Depository, CreateSpace, OZON.ru, and Barnes and Noble.

ISBN: 978-1491297100 (English); ISBN: 978-3868735925 (German);
ISBN: 978-5916712681 (Russian); ISBN: 978-1494247768 (Spanish)

Visit www.atlasofprejudice.com for more information.